BEREAVED PARENTS AND
THEIR CONTINUING BONDS

of related interest

A Matter of Life and Death
60 Voices Share their Wisdom
Rosalind Bradley
Foreword by Archbishop Emeritus Desmond Tutu
ISBN 978 1 84905 601 4
eISBN 978 1 78450 283 6

The Essential Guide to Life After Bereavement
Beyond Tomorrow
Judy Carole Kauffmann and Mary Jordan
ISBN 978 1 84905 335 8
eISBN 978 0 85700 669 1

Supporting People through Loss and Grief
An Introduction for Counsellors and Other Caring Practitioners
John Wilson
ISBN 978 1 84905 376 1
eISBN 978 0 85700 739 1

Setting Up and Facilitating Bereavement Support Groups
A Practical Guide
Dodie Graves
ISBN 978 1 84905 271 9
eISBN 978 0 85700 573 1

I'll Write Your Name on Every Beach
A Mother's Quest for Comfort, Courage and Clarity After Suicide Loss
Susan Auerbach
ISBN 978 1 78592 758 4
eISBN 978 1 78450 615 5

BEREAVED PARENTS AND THEIR CONTINUING BONDS

Love after Death

Catherine Seigal

Jessica Kingsley *Publishers*
London and Philadelphia

Epigraph on page 15 reprinted by permission of HarperCollins Publishers
Ltd © Julie Nicholson 2011. Epigraph on page 73 reprinted from McCracken
2009 by permission of Jonathan Cape. Epigraph on page 88 reprinted from
Jenkins 2016 by permission of Mererid Hopwood © 2016. Story on page 117
reprinted by kind permission of Guardian News and Media Ltd © 2017.

First published in 2017
by Jessica Kingsley Publishers
73 Collier Street
London N1 9BE, UK
and
400 Market Street, Suite 400
Philadelphia, PA 19106, USA

www.jkp.com

Copyright © Catherine Seigal 2017

Library of Congress Cataloging in Publication Data
A CIP catalog record for this book is available from the Library of Congress

British Library Cataloguing in Publication Data
A CIP catalogue record for this book is available from the British Library

ISBN 978 1 78592 326 5
eISBN 978 1 78450 641 4

Printed and bound by CPI Group (UK) Ltd, Croydon, CR0 4YY

This book is dedicated to all the parents I had the privilege of meeting and working with when I was a counsellor at a children's hospital. What you taught me has stayed with me in a way no book on counselling theory ever could. Thank you for allowing me to be alongside you during that very difficult and dark period of your lives.

It is also dedicated to your children, knowing that your love for them continues forever.

ACKNOWLEDGEMENTS

I am indebted to all those who have contributed directly and indirectly to the book, especially the parents who shared their stories with me and my many inspiring colleagues who taught me so much about compassion.

My thanks go to Mollie Cook who was the first person to tell me I should write this book, to Andrew Cooper and Denise Turner who have been so encouraging along the way, Matt and Anna Shipton for formatting and full stops, Stuart and Sue Nuttall and their team together with Tim Posner for producing the video to promote my book, everyone at Jessica Kingsley Publishers, with a special mention for Emily Badger, editorial assistant, who has been most helpful to this novice author, and my husband who has been very patient, reading and re-reading and positive from the beginning.

CONTENTS

Disclaimer 8

Introduction 9

1. Establishing the Bond through Place, in a
    Changed Landscape 15

2. Nurturing the Bond through Talking: The Role
    of Counselling 27

3. Creating the Bond when There Has Been so
    Little Time Together 37

4. How a Group Can Strengthen the Bond 48

5. Beginning the Transition: Spiritual Meanings and the
    Continuing Bond 59

6. The Place of Ritual in Maintaining and Nourishing the Bond . 73

7. Holding on to the Bond when Another Child Is Born 81

8. How Brothers and Sisters Help Parents Strengthen the Bond . . 88

9. What Might Get in the Way of Parents Being Able to Establish
    a Continuing Bond? 98

10. Can the Continuing Bond Be a Source of New Energy
    and Strength? 115

11. Working as a Counsellor with Bereaved Parents 122

References 137

Resources. 139

DISCLAIMER

In order to protect the confidentiality of the families I have written about I have taken care to disguise their identities and have not named the hospital where I worked.

The parents I have been able to reach have been encouraging and generously given their consent to be included. I have altered their names, their children's names and ages and family make-up, except where they have asked me not to. Sometimes I have changed the reason their child died. Parents I haven't been able to reach to ask for their consent, I have disguised even more fully, with parts of their story fictionalised. I do not think that this has in any way diminished the authenticity of their experiences as described in this book.

INTRODUCTION

Circles of sorrow mark my course.

Gluck, *Iphigénie en Tauride* (1779)

In the chapel of a teaching hospital in London, at the east end, there is an area dedicated to the memory of children who have died. Above the book of remembrance, where these children are named, a patchwork quilt hangs. It was sewn by a group of women who wanted to make something to personalise and enhance this small area of a large chapel in a very big hospital.

We asked recently bereaved parents to suggest images they would like to see included: what would bring their children to mind, and possibly also bring a smile. There are embroidered rainbows and stars, butterflies and sunrays. Somewhere there is a frog and a mobile phone and a multi-coloured elephant. Patchwork tells stories, and this quilt captures something of the many stories of the children who are remembered at the hospital.

And this writing too I think is rather like that. It is a patchwork of stories of children who have died that their families have shared with me. And just as the individual pictures make the whole, which is in itself a story, so I have tried to draw from these personal stories a bigger understanding of how it is that parents are gently able to finely embroider an ongoing relationship with their child who is no longer in this world.

What I have written is drawn from my time working as a counsellor with parents who had experienced the death of their child. For five years I was a counsellor at a children's hospital which is part of a London teaching hospital. Together with a colleague I offered a service to parents whose children were patients at the hospital. This service was available to all parents, but a very important part of it was the counselling service to parents whose child had died in the hospital, or whose child had been cared for by the hospital but who died elsewhere, possibly in a children's hospice, another hospital or at home. I use the term 'parents' to include a child's full-time carer who may not be the biological parent. When I refer to a child in the singular I write 'she' rather than the more clumsy 'he or she'.

The thoughts and feelings I have set down come for the greater part from the parents I sat alongside over this time. They spoke with me on the wards, in the counselling room, in the group I facilitated, on the phone and as we encountered each other in the hospital corridors. Since I retired from this work in 2013 their voices have continued to speak to me. It hasn't been possible to forget them and I haven't wanted to. I owe these parents so much; they taught me everything I now hold to be relevant about bereavement work. And I believe I owe it to them to write some of it down both for other professionals to read, and maybe also for bereaved parents to draw from.

Crucially I learned that no theory of grief or loss fits the experience that was being described to me. Nothing could capture adequately the truly dreadful, chaotic, contradictory, overwhelming place parents find themselves inhabiting following the death of their child. It is certainly not a journey, though too easily we can use this word. Journey implies a direction and a possible destination. For many parents there is neither.

The first twentieth-century writers to begin to make sense of the grieving process made the whole messy, bewildering experience more understandable and manageable by assigning a task for the bereaved, which was to disengage from the relationship with the person who had died. They then described phases the griever passed through, or tasks that were accomplished as they moved towards the eventual acceptance of their loss and the internalisation of the loved one who had died. Over the years these theories have been helpful both to the bereaved and those who care for them. First of all death and how we suffer when we lose someone became something that could be spoken about. In addition the confusing and sometimes frightening feelings grievers described were seen as normal and understandable, and perhaps most importantly of all, there was the suggestion of a time-line; however distressed people felt, for most the pain would eventually lessen and they could begin to look forward to a time when they would feel at peace again.

But recent writers in the field of bereavement have been questioning the helpfulness of seeing grieving as task orientated. There has been a concern that these theories can be interpreted rigidly, and that sometimes the individual experience of grief can get lost. And, in particular, for parents who lose a child, ideas of stages or phases in the grief process, tasks that are addressed and accomplished, and the very prospect of some kind of resolution...none of this feels real or at all relevant. Celia Hindmarch, a counsellor with years of experience of working with bereaved families at the Alder Hey bereavement support project in Liverpool, was one of the first writers to address this, and in her book *On the Death of a Child* writes, 'Conventional theories of grief have been found inadequate when it comes to the death of a child' (Hindmarch 2009, p.30).

Bereaved parents often have a considerable investment in continuing to grieve, and fear the day their pain will ease even to a small degree. They are afraid it could signify a weakening of their attachment to their child. It can feel like a betrayal. It could herald a fading of memories, so closely treasured and drawn from.

Critically, what these more recent writers have done is to suggest that mourning was not about relinquishing the bonds with the person who has died but about finding new and different ways of sustaining them.

For parents who lose a child, this means that there is an enduring relationship between themselves and their grief. They are always walking alongside it. The most resolution there can be is only as much as a parent's grief can ever allow; their child will remain in their heart, mind and being for all time. The loss will have changed them, they will never return to how they were before and life will never be the same again. But there is more than that; their child's life will continue to have meaning.

Hindmarch describes it this way:

> There is one resource that is easily overlooked, and this is the source of strength that comes from the bereaved parents' continuing relationship with the child after death. This does not require a belief in the spirit world or an afterlife, but recognition that every life, however short or limited, leaves its mark. (Hindmarch 2009, p.190)

Bereaved parents don't deny the physical death of their child but are able to form a continuing bond with that child who lives within them. From my conversations with bereaved parents I would add that the internalised child also continues to influence and inform the parents' view of the world, their plans for themselves, their families and their passions in the future.

Perhaps at this point it is important to write that many bereaved parents ask themselves the question, 'Should I keep on living now my child has died?'

When a parent loses a child it is not uncommon for them to have thoughts about ending their own lives, particularly in the early days, but later on too, especially at anniversaries, birthdays and Christmas, or special family days like Mother's and Father's Day. For most parents there are times when life would be easier if it were no longer lived. Living with such intense, unremitting anguish can be hard to bear. Jayson Greene wrote in *The Sunday Times* about the sudden death of his two-year-old daughter Greta:

> When I realized Greta would not live, I wanted to die so purely and so simply. I could feel my heart gazing up at me quizzically, asking me in between beats: 'Are you sure you want me to keep doing this?' But I found I could not give the order. (Greene 2016, p.22)

Some parents may also hold a belief or hope that to die would mean to be reunited with their child. But for most there are reasons to carry on: other children to be born or to care for, tasks to be done that will honour the child who has died, partners, family and friends to hold and comfort, systems to be fought, diseases to be researched and eradicated...

A parent's love is a love that is stronger than death.

Through my work as a counsellor and facilitating a bereaved parents' group I began to think more about the bonds that continue between parent and child after death. I wanted to understand more about how parents create this precious bond, and about the bond itself. Would the bond be different when parents lose a child at birth or in the first few weeks of life from those who had lost their child later in childhood or as a teenager? I wondered how the bond might be if the child who died had been previously well and had died unexpectedly, and whether it differed if the child had been born with a life-limiting condition.

So it was with this in mind that I began to think through some of the conversations I had with the parents I worked with. How is it possible for parents to nurture and be nurtured by a continuing relationship with their child who is no longer alive? How do parents continue to experience this relationship – how do they describe it? What strengthens this bond and what are the challenges to it? Is every bond unique or are there commonly held experiences about what this bond is like? How conscious is the process of developing this bond?

I became interested in whether the ongoing bond changed if there was another child born subsequent to the death, and whether it differed for parents who had other children from those who had lost their only child.

What I write is not backed by empirical research. It is a descriptive account of what the parents spoke about and how I understood it.

Chapter 1

ESTABLISHING THE BOND THROUGH PLACE, IN A CHANGED LANDSCAPE

How can everything still appear so normal and unchanged when our whole world has changed? I want to scream at the crowds in the street and groups hurrying in and out of Waterstones: Don't you know what's happened? How can you go about your lives so normally when our world has collapsed?

> Julie Nicholson, *A Song for Jenny: A Mother's Story of Love and Loss* (2011), written after her daughter was killed in the London bombings on 7 July 2005

When your child dies it can feel as if the world you once inhabited has changed beyond recognition and will never again return to how it was. Parents speak about it no longer being the safe, predictable, reliable place they knew, and when the death is sudden and unexpected this can be more so. 'When I am on the playground years from now, watching my son take a fall from the monkey bars, I may not panic. But some part of me will remember: a heartbeat can stop' (Greene 2016, p.22).

This strange new world can start, of course, before a child dies, when they become unwell and suddenly everything is different. In his book *Do No Harm*, Henry Marsh, a consultant neurosurgeon, writes about the time his child became extremely unwell and was admitted to hospital:

My wife and I spent the next few weeks in that strange world one enters when you fear for your child's life – the outside world, the real world, becomes a ghost world and the people in it remote and indistinct. The only reality is intense fear, a fear driven by helpless overwhelming love. (Marsh 2014, p.108)

Recounting the isolation period known as 'going to green' at the Spanish hospital where the writer Sergio del Molino's little boy was receiving chemotherapy for infant leukaemia, del Molino writes:

Going to green imposes a military discipline on us, far worse than anything we have lived through until now, and we bear it because we know that we are now on the part of the map that is inhabited by monsters. Creatures that no one has ever seen but that eat ships and valiant sailors. (del Molino 2013, p.68)

Marsh's child recovers; del Molino's child does not. For parents whose children do not get better, the world outside remains changed, hostile and unknown, and eventually they have to find a way to re-enter it.

We all hold, often unconsciously, core beliefs about the reliability and safety of the world, and usually our experience of life strengthens and supports these beliefs. When we are presented with unexpected and difficult experiences we find ways of managing and integrating the challenges these give to our core beliefs, without our basic trust in the world being compromised.

But sometimes what happens is so traumatic that the beliefs we hold are shattered. Rules we once trusted and lived by have been broken and we no longer feel safe. When parents lose a child they will sometimes describe a feeling that there are no longer any certainties in life. Moreover, the protective skin that enabled them to live a happy and meaningful life has been stripped away, and they are left feeling vulnerable and anxious. For many this protective skin will have already taken a battering through the long days, months and sometimes years of caring for a sick child – of hopes being raised and disappointed, and of times when it seemed that nothing would ever feel certain again.

Perceptions of time can also change. Stuart told me that since his son Toby died he sees his life in two distinct parts – the time when Toby was alive and the time after he died:

> When I place memories I put them into one or the other part, before or after. The second part has been robbed of what I can only describe as joy. So there is happiness and laughter and good times but ultimately no joy, because joy doesn't have any constraint on it, and after the death of your child there is always a constraint and a check.

For del Molino, describing his emotional journey through the diagnosis, treatment and then death of Pablo, not only the present and the projected future become irrevocably changed, but the past and how he perceived himself are no longer the same:

> The past is a long way away, and memory fades among the days and nights spent in the hospital. My past belongs to someone else, and it's more and more difficult for me to give him a face. What did he feel, what did he like to do, what made him laugh, this unknown man who once had a son called Pablo? (del Molino 2013, pp.104–105)

And he writes how experiences and memories of the past are now altered by this new present, 'a file that has suddenly become volatile. Folders and folders filled with visions of an impossible yesterday' (del Molino 2013, p.61).

As parents look out at this altered landscape, the world can literally not even look the same. One father, Marvin, spoke of it now appearing as if the colour had drained out of it. A mother, Rose, spoke of seeing it as a pale watercolour, where previously it had been a vibrant oil painting.

The world has become a place where the darkest fears have come true and parents can feel fearful about their own and others' safety and wellbeing. Janet spoke about being no longer able to drive along country lanes at night and Zoe became highly anxious if her husband was late home from work. Terrible things have happened and can happen again. The laws of probability have changed.

But as well as the landscape being different, familiar things have changed too. Home is no longer the same, relationships in the family and in the community have altered, and others behave differently with you. Parents have to redefine who they are in the context of the loss of their social role and their identity as this child's parent. They are, for this child, no longer a physical carer, an encourager, provider and educator, and a safe place. They will have to withdraw the hopes and expectations they had held about their future life with their child. For those who lose their only child, parents have to work out whether they can now even refer to themselves as a mother or father.

Our society has a name for those who lose a partner – a widow or widower – and a child who loses both parents is an orphan. But we have no word for a parent who loses a child. It is interesting that in China, where from the 1980s until 2015 there was a one-child policy, the loss of the only child is seen as so devastating that a name is given to bereaved parents. They are called *Shidu fumu*.

The world has changed, the parents' role within it has changed, and they know too they are changed within. When a child dies, parents can feel that they have lost a part of themselves, and the feeling of being incomplete and empty may not go away. It is experienced in a very physical way. Some describe it as an emptiness that can never be filled; others liken it to a severing of a part of the body. Harriet, who lost her daughter at six days, knew with absolute clarity that she would 'never stop grieving' because her grief had become 'part of my body'.

Bereaved parents have now to work out different ways of speaking to others about themselves.

'What do I say when people ask how many children I have?'

The simplest answer a parent can give is the number of living children. But this can feel like a betrayal of the child who has died. How can it be that they no longer count and are counted? But it can become complicated for a parent who responds with a number that includes the child who has died. When further questions are asked it can emerge that one child is no longer alive, and parents then find themselves having to explain more than they may have wanted or felt like doing. Sometimes the nature of the interaction does not call for this kind of disclosure.

So parents are caught; do they 'lie' and feel like they are betraying their child or do they find themselves unwillingly drawn into a deep and complex conversation with someone who they may never encounter again? What was once a straightforward piece of social intercourse has become fraught and complicated.

One mother, having taken part in a conversation about this issue in the group I facilitated, concluded, 'I feel as if I have lost my innocence.' She had indeed. Not knowing whether to tell strangers that she had one child or none was one uncertainty in a life that had changed forever for this young mother, Tammy. When she became pregnant for the first time with her daughter, Emily, Tammy had no thought that this would not end happily. But as she progressed through her pregnancy, concerns for her unborn child grew, with scans showing a severe heart abnormality. Emily lived just a few hours and Tammy's view of the world being a good and kind place collapsed. Life before Emily had been happy, straightforward and predictable. Tammy's experience was that if you did the right things you were usually guaranteed a good outcome. Now there were no longer these certainties. She was young and healthy, she hadn't smoked or drank alcohol during the pregnancy, had attended antenatal classes and prepared a nursery. And yet Emily had died.

The world Tammy had looked forward to sharing with Emily no longer existed. Tammy had to find a way of continuing to live and find meaning, and to connect with a child she had only really known when she was in her womb. This was a challenge she rose to with admirable spirit and determination, committing herself to supporting a charity which offered support and financial help to families who had a child with a heart condition. Although she had no living child, she called herself a mother. And her partner was a father. They had created a child together and given birth. This was their certainty in an uncertain world.

But it is not only the way the world is perceived that changes: it *is* no longer as it was, and this can present some difficult challenges for parents. When Tina and Mark's daughter Sophie died suddenly of viral meningitis at the age of ten, Tina found it really hard to return to her daughter's school. This was problematic because Sophie's younger brother still attended and needed taking and collecting. Tina had to face the playground and other parents daily and she found it unbearable; not that other parents were unfriendly or avoided her, though at times they were visibly awkward. What was especially upsetting for Tina was to see her daughter's contemporaries. How could they be continuing their lives as if nothing had changed? Tina would search out and see Sophie's face amongst the crowd, and hear her voice amongst the voices of the other children. As time passed it didn't get any easier, and only when Sophie's contemporaries moved on to secondary school did the playground become less of an ordeal.

For other families, though, an ongoing relationship with their child's friends and school can feel supportive, and help them feel close to their child. When Ahmed died from sudden heart failure at the age of fifteen, the football team of which he had been a member worked hard to raise money for a heart charity in memory of their friend. Ahmed's family were involved in the planning and events, and valued spending time with these young people who reminded them of their son.

When a baby dies before birth or in the first few weeks it is painful for the new mother to meet up with the women who had been part of her pregnancy network, such as those she had got to know in her hospital antenatal classes or National Childbirth Trust antenatal group. And these women in turn, most of whom will now have healthy babies, will find it hard to know what to say or do. Usually the bereaved mother will find it easier not to meet up, even though this can feel like losing friends. Others will take comfort in new networks of support, possibly through Sands, the UK stillbirth and neonatal death charity and support group (see the Resources section at the end of this book).

But this is not the same for everyone. Tammy found nothing more touching and comforting than when a friend from her antenatal group placed in her arms her own newborn baby, only days after Tammy's baby had died. She felt the ache of her empty arms soothed.

So there are no rules, no absolutes. If Tammy's friend had not taken that risk, Tammy would have missed out on a real source of comfort. Yet for another mother this gesture would have been experienced as insensitive and thoughtless. Perhaps all that can be said is that friends, colleagues and family members can only ask, and try to find a way to be alongside that person in their sadness.

Parents whose children have had a longstanding illness or disability also lose an extensive network of social relationships and routines when their child dies. There will be the carers and therapists who supported their child and the close and significant relationships with doctors and hospital staff. There is the loss of the regular appointments and, when the child has been in hospital for long periods, the relationships with other parents on the wards. Many parents of children with disabilities speak about the full-time job of arranging and arguing for the best and most appropriate services for their child's needs. This will have had frustrations, but now is no longer necessary. And, of course, there is always, for parents of children with or without disabilities, the loss of all that comes with being the parent of a child who needs care.

When a child with disabilities has required adaptations, equipment and supplies in the home, it can be upsetting to see these taken away. Parents usually need some time to pass before they can contemplate letting go of or changing their child's room, but for those whose home and child's room housed equipment supplied by the local community services, there is no choice about when it is removed. At times it is almost callously soon that arrangements are made for the removal of wheelchairs, feeding pumps, hoists and adapted beds. These things were very much part of the child's everyday life, and as such imbued with meaning for parents. Anne's baby Aimee needed special feeding bottles. After she died Anne continued to keep one in the kitchen. It reminded her of the long hours she would sit holding her little girl helping her feed.

In this altered landscape some parents found returning to the hospital where their child had been cared for, and perhaps also where their child had died, helpful in strengthening an ongoing connection with their child.

Victoria and John's son Alexander died at the age of eleven. From birth he had been severely disabled by seizures and towards the end of his life spent long periods as an inpatient whilst doctors tried to control his seizures and severe movement disorders. Together with his parents and grandparents, this little boy, who enchanted all who knew him, was well known by many of the hospital staff. Alexander spent the Christmas before he died in hospital and his extended family were part of the celebrations. Many of the staff who had cared for Alexander came to his funeral, and his occupational therapist read a poem she had written for him.

Not long after Alexander died his father came to me for counselling. He deeply valued the opportunity to be back in the place where his son had been so known and loved, and which had played a hugely significant part in Alexander's life. It helped too that I had known his son. John saw the counselling as time set aside to remember Alexander, something that became especially treasured, as his life became busier over the subsequent months with a demanding job and the birth of a child. But it was the remembering of his son in this place, which had belonged to Alexander, that felt significant. He felt especially close to Alexander when he was in the hospital. Victoria was offered counselling with my colleague, but she found returning to the hospital distressing. Her GP arranged counselling for her through the surgery.

Evelyn's daughter Katy died in hospital after she was admitted at the age of twelve months with what was found to be a complex mitochondrial condition, and she stayed on the ward until she died. For Evelyn, although the hospital had been the place where she had faced the agony of losing her first child, it was also the place where she and her precious daughter had spent their final weeks together. Unencumbered by the routine tasks of running a home, Evelyn was able to devote herself entirely to her child, sitting at her cot-side watching her whilst she slept, or holding her in her arms when awake. After Katy died and Evelyn had returned to work, she would choose to lengthen her journey home by travelling on a bus that went past the hospital.

Children having renal dialysis will usually come to the hospital three days a week, often for several years. Together with their parents they build close attachments to the ward and the staff, who become like family. There are also relationships built with other families. For the parents of a child who dies and who has been a dialysis patient, the ending of this connection to both place and people can feel immense. For some a return visit brings company and the comfort of the familiar, but inevitably as time passes, staff, families and systems change, and the place begins to feel less familiar.

At the hospital where I worked bereaved parents and their families are invited to a Time to Remember service which is held twice a year. Organised by the chaplaincy and the counsellors, it gives families an opportunity to remember the child they have lost through music and readings. Returning to the hospital for this is helpful for many parents, who do not have to explain their visit but are welcomed as guests. Here their children are remembered in a place where they were known and cared for. Here too are others who have the same reasons for being there. Continuity of the staff helps parents feel the institution still holds them in mind. Some parents attend these events for many years after their child's death.

As well as the hospital playing a significant part in the continuing bond between parent and child, for some parents the parents' accommodation was important as well. James and Nathalie stayed in the parents' accommodation for several weeks whilst their daughter Jenny was cared for on the paediatric intensive care unit. Previously a well child, she had developed a complex lung condition at the age of eighteen months, and was never well enough to return home. For James and Nathalie, the parents' accommodation became the home they returned to every night, where staff and other parents listened to their fears and sorrow. Although this was a desperate period in their lives, the house offered these parents warmth and a sanctuary, and their child was known there, even though she never came in person. After Jenny died James and Nathalie continued to draw on the comfort they had found at the parents' accommodation by attending the parents' group I held there. Two years on Nathalie became a volunteer at the house, not only because she had the experience and sensitivity to support other parents, as she had been supported, but also because being there reminded her of those final months with Jenny, which had been both bitter and sweet.

But for some parents the ongoing bond with their child is not strengthened by a relationship with the hospital. For them the hospital is a place where their worst fears were realised. For these parents future connections to the hospital are usually traumatic and to be avoided. My sense is that parents who felt this way tended to be those whose child had suffered a sudden and unexpected death, or those who believed that the hospital failed their child. For parents whose time at the hospital had been brief, there had been little opportunity to form relationships with staff, and their experience was that, however competent and kind they were, they would always be associated with the most terrible moments of life.

Alisha, a three-month-old baby, became suddenly and acutely unwell at home. An ambulance took her and her parents to the Accident and Emergency department at the hospital, but by the time she had arrived she had stopped breathing. Resuscitation was not successful, and Alisha died before she could be taken to a ward. Her parents stayed with their little girl for a few hours before saying goodbye, and whilst staff took her to the mortuary they returned home, to the place where earlier that day everything had been normal. These parents found it extremely difficult to have anything more to do with the hospital, and were unable to contemplate returning, either to see their daughter, to have a follow-up meeting with the consultant, or to use any of the services offered by the counsellors. Their connection with the hospital was entirely to do with the feelings of shock, pain and horror. It had become a place they would never want to see again. For these parents, as for Victoria, local counselling services accessed through the GP or through local child bereavement organisations were more acceptable.

Chapter 2

NURTURING THE BOND THROUGH TALKING: THE ROLE OF COUNSELLING

Remembering takes me back to that moment all over again.

Parent of Lily, who died at birth

Most parents have a strong desire to talk about their child who has died. This is not always easy as sometimes others do not feel they can listen. Parents describe experiences of awkwardness when they encounter family, friends and neighbours after their child has died. Sometimes people will cross the road to avoid a difficult conversation with a bereaved parent.

Close friends and family are almost always supportive, but to be continuously exposed to someone's pain can be hard. Bereaved parents may sense this and censor what they speak about and how much they say. Friends and family long to see their distraught relative or friend showing signs of feeling better. At times they will blame themselves for being unable to help. Others may express their impatience and suggest that it is 'time to move on', advice which is never helpful or welcome, or indeed carries any meaning.

The counselling service at the hospital offered parents one-to-one and couple counselling. Within the constraints of the service and the need to manage client waiting times, we tried to offer an unlimited number of sessions, arranged in whatever way parents found most helpful: weekly, fortnightly, monthly, or simply when it was requested.

That is not to say we had no input into how the sessions were organised. As counsellors it was our responsibility to sometimes suggest a parent came for their next session sooner than they were considering, and we also had a responsibility to help parents to finish their work with us. But within that there was freedom for parents to use our sessions as they needed to. It was important to give them the opportunity to speak at length and over some considerable time. It was also important for them to know that we understood that they might need to say the same things, to tell the same stories, over and over.

Some parents valued and settled into the longer-term counselling relationship that was on offer. Jane, whose daughter died from a congenital heart condition, came for her first session within a month of her daughter's death. She continued to come weekly until she returned to work, when she changed to fortnightly sessions. Before the birth of her third child we met more frequently and then she took a break for two months, after which she continued for a further two years with monthly appointments. Our relationship spanned a long and significant period of Jane's life, moving from the shock and tragedy of the earlier period, when her need to meet was intense, through the limitations set by a return to work, and then a period of increased anxiety during her pregnancy, and eventually a gradual ending as life with two healthy children took over.

Ian came for a very intense short period of weekly counselling following the tragic and unexpected death of his son in a road traffic accident. Three months after his son's death he went back to work full time and the counselling ended. He felt he needed to 'box up' the time with me and return to the familiar routines of home and work. This gave him the structure he needed to manage both his pain and the demands of his life.

Jenny and Peter's little boy Nicky died at home after a local hospital missed a presentation of bacterial meningitis and sent him home from the Accident and Emergency department. The family were referred to our services because they didn't feel able to return to their local hospital but were desperately in need of support. Jenny and her husband came together for the first two sessions, but Peter found speaking about what had happened too distressing, so Jenny continued to attend alone. With three other children at home and an increasingly depressed partner, she often cancelled her sessions, and at other times would phone and ask to be seen as quickly as possible. Her need to talk was on an 'as and when' basis, and to be able to respond to that was important.

Three very different clients, who shared a strong desire and need to talk to someone outside the network of family and friends about the child they had lost. For each this was arranged in a way that fitted in with their life and their perception of what they needed. Each was clear that the opportunity to speak to a counsellor was a way of connecting with their child. In counselling they had the undivided attention of a person who would listen carefully and thoughtfully, often to the same material spoken again and again. A counsellor is not someone who directs the conversation or points out that a story has been heard before. She won't flinch or appear uncomfortable when descriptions are given of the moment of death and the times passed with the dead child. Over time, a counsellor may facilitate the sharing of further memories and experiences through sensitive questioning. With experience, a counsellor is able to emotionally hold someone who is distraught and broken, without feeling overwhelmed or anxious, and enable a parent to feel sufficiently strong to leave the room at the end of the session and return to their life.

Of course, it doesn't always work like that. There were times when as a counsellor I recognised that I wasn't feeling quite so robust and may well have conveyed that to a parent. Other times a powerful human wish to offer comfort and reassurance prematurely can interfere, and a parent can fear that their feelings are too big for the counsellor to manage. On occasions I misjudged a parent's readiness and need to talk about very difficult things, and they felt too hurried and withdrew. For all practising counsellors supervision is essential. In this work I knew that the high-quality, honest and regular supervision I received was critical to my being able to manage hearing very distressing stories day after day.

There were parents who came for counselling but were unsure whether it would be helpful, and who, having found themselves with me, felt that it was not helpful to talk; perhaps it was all too soon or too frightening, I wasn't the right person, or I didn't offer the advice they were looking for.

Jan McLaren, a counsellor who worked with families at The Laura Centre, a bereavement service in Leicester, writes about something she terms 'the invisible therapist syndrome'. She describes how in the early stages of working with bereaved parents she often has a sense that she is invisible; that the 'mutual interactive relationship' she usually experienced with clients just isn't happening. She suggests that what is occurring mirrors what is happening in the parents' other relationships; that 'grieving parents are so immersed in thoughts, feelings and memories of the dead child they are unable to be fully present to any others' (McLaren 1998, p.283). However, as parents emerge from this preoccupation, they are able to engage more with a therapeutic relationship and with the world in general.

I wonder whether this process is not unlike what happens in the relationship with a mother and her newborn infant, what the psychotherapist D.W. Winnicott called 'primary maternal preoccupation'. In the early weeks of a child's life, if circumstances allow, a mother is able to adapt her entire self to being responsive to the needs of her baby. It is almost as if she is in a state of reverie; the outside world takes second place to her absorption in the symbiotic relationship with her infant. This is the key to the formation of a secure bond with her baby (Winnicott 1990). When a child dies, it may be that this earlier state is revisited because the mother needs and desires to reconnect with that powerful early attachment to her child, in order to renegotiate separation.

Where that leaves fathers is interesting. Winnicott's view is that at the beginning of the infant's life, it is the father's emotional holding of the mother which supports her and enables her to enter into this exclusive and all-consuming relationship (Winnicott 2000). And, for some, maybe it is so after death. Generally, but certainly not always, it was my experience that fathers were less preoccupied by their loss; not less affected, but less absorbed by ruminations about it. This could be seen as men tending to be less expressive of their feelings, but I wonder if it could also be understood in terms of them, unconsciously perhaps, recognising their role in holding the mother in her grief.

Over time parents who did commit to counselling, and who came and talked, and shared stories of their child's life and death, found counselling played a special part in nurturing the bond between themselves and their child.

Telling stories of their child's life, in the context of it now having ended, gives the stories a new perspective and dimension. This can bring both joy and sadness. There is the pleasure of remembering and recounting the story, for at that moment of telling it can seem as if the child is alive again; then follows the reality and the accompanying knowing that the child is no longer living. Telling a story can change it, and this changed version then has to be reflected upon, and taken in.

Thelma spoke about a birthday she had celebrated earlier that year, with her daughter Jesse and two older children. She was a single parent for whom money was often short. Her children had secretly saved pocket money over the preceding weeks to pay for the four of them to go to the cinema on her birthday. This plan came as a complete surprise, and Thelma was touched and delighted that her children had thought up a celebration they could all enjoy together. Tragically, just three weeks later Jesse died unexpectedly from a virus that overwhelmed her immune system. Thelma experienced both great joy and terrible pain in recounting the cinema trip in its every detail, moment by moment. In the telling of it she remembered and treasured again the pleasure of this lovely gift, but in the context of it having become her last birthday before Jesse died and one of the last things the family did together as a complete family, the perspective of the story changed. There was an underscoring of tragedy, Jesse's thoughtfulness became more highly valued and admired, and the memory of the outing became highly emotionally loaded.

When Jenny first shared with me the account of the visit to Accident and Emergency at their local hospital with Nicky, she told me the bare facts. When she could contain her cries of anger and pain for a moment, she described her experience of the hospital being understaffed and under-resourced, of not being heard and their child not being properly attended to. Each time Jenny and I met she told this story, and as the months passed her account developed and changed. The facts remained the same, but more was added. She began to speak of the nurse who had tried to get more help for them and had been concerned that they were being told to take Nicky home. She spoke about how frightened Nicky had seemed and the words he had spoken to her and his daddy as they waited for a doctor to see him. She spoke about the Christmas decorations that were up in the hospital, and how someone had brought her a cup of tea. She remembered how white her little boy had looked, as they wrapped him in a blanket to carry him out to the car park. She wondered about why she and her partner had said so little when they were deeply concerned to be told to take Nicky home. She remembered the music that they played in the car on the drive home. One week she finally was able to speak to me about how, later that evening, whilst she was upstairs checking on the other children, her partner had called out, and she had gone downstairs to find him holding the lifeless body of their precious child. And then Jenny told me the story again.

Telling the story and growing the story is finding a way to take in the enormity of what has happened. As the words are spoken and returned to, the story becomes more part of who the teller is. Shared with someone else and reflected upon together, it is deepened, carved into the heart and mind. It becomes a vital seam in the bond that unites parent and child. And somehow, over time, the telling of it can become softer and sadder, less angry and anguished.

And for the telling to be helpful parents need a listener who can help them articulate their unbearable feelings. Describing her work with bereaved mothers on a neonatal intensive care unit, Cohen writes, 'Most people need the presence of an external person to give voice to their feelings – someone who is at least trying to understand' (Cohen 2003, p.129).

As the counsellor listens to clients describe their experiences, the counselling relationship mirrors the earlier infantile relationships when others caring for us, usually parents, help us to recognise and name what had been previously unarticulated feelings. In the security of a good counselling relationship parents are able to return to that early developmental task of naming and then knowing and owning feelings that are so new and distressing they feel terrifying. Through helping parents process what has happened to them, these new narratives nurture the developing bond between parent and child.

Telling the story of what happened to their child to other people is something most parents want to be able to do. They want to find a way of saying what happened in words that convey enough but also convey that there is, and always will be, more. And also that the words used may not always be the right words but, for now, they are all that can be spoken.

There are times when we struggle to wrap words around things that happen to us, maybe because they are too wonderful for words, maybe because they are too terrible. In counselling parents might be silent or they might search for words and speak them aloud to test out whether they sound right: whether they truly express what they need them to. Parents' narratives need to be gently and carefully constructed and rehearsed.

I learned through listening to parents as they told their child's story how important it was for them to be in control of the content. They welcomed hearing others speak about their child, but only when they invited it.

After Freddie died his parents were invited back to his school to attend a special assembly where his classmates shared paintings and writing they had done about their friend. The staff had prepared a video of Freddie taken from film they had made of all the children whilst in school: in a singing class, playing outside and dancing. Freddie's parents, though touched by the staff's kindness, found it so upsetting to watch new images of Freddie that they had not previously known about. They felt unprepared and were distressed watching, in a public place, some narratives about Freddie that were not their own.

It is important for counsellors to judge how far to help parents, who are feeling so fragile and vulnerable, to be in touch with their feelings within the time constraints of a session. At the end of a session parents have to leave and face a world where there may be less understanding and sensitivity, and where lives are continuing as if nothing had changed. However deeply parents allowed me to see their pain, I needed to find a way of enabling them to touch a source of strength before they left the room; I might ask about who would be there for them when they returned home, or how they would look after themselves for the rest of that day. In this way I hoped to convey that I knew the day ahead was likely to be hard, but at the same time was confident they would manage.

Meriel came to see me following the death of her three-year-old son. She was a Muslim and her face and body were covered. After a tentative beginning, expressing her uncertainty about how much she wanted to talk, she stood up and removed her niqab, a veil that covered her face, and abaya, the loose-fitting garment that covered her body. Underneath she was wearing jeans and a jumper. Then she relaxed and began to talk, and perhaps I relaxed too. When it was time to leave she covered herself again.

I only saw her once and she made a profound impression. She made me think about how all the people I see will to some extent have an experience of disrobing – of removing a protective covering – and how important it is that they can put it on again when they leave. Sometimes I would see it in the way a parent would spend time before they went out of the door, slowly putting on a coat and buttoning it, wrapping a scarf around their neck, and checking and packing their bag. It was important not to be impatient and to allow this preparation to meet a world that has turned hard and cold.

Looking back on the counselling sessions with these parents I find it interesting to remember that mostly I learned little about their early history. My previous counselling work and training had been strongly influenced by the importance of understanding what the client brought to the work in the context of knowing something about their early childhood experiences. But working with bereaved parents, the story they brought of their lost child was enough. After ten, twenty, thirty sessions, there was always more to talk about.

Chapter 3

CREATING THE BOND WHEN THERE HAS BEEN SO LITTLE TIME TOGETHER

Life and death are neighbours nigh.

> Thomas Hardy, 'Nature's Questioning', in
> *Wessex Poems and Other Verses* (1898)

In the bereaved parents' group I ran, one of the conversations parents had from time to time was 'Is it different for a parent when a child dies at birth or in the first few days or when a child dies in childhood or later?' My response, not voiced, would be that it appeared to me that it was different for all parents, whatever the age of their child. However, the group would return to this question with an honesty and frankness which these parents seemed to be able to have with each other. They were always curious about each other's experiences.

Often those who had lost an older child would say something along the lines of 'I think it must be harder for parents who lose a child early in life because they have had so little time together, and so few memories to draw from.' Those who had lost a child early in life would then respond, suggesting that 'Perhaps it was not harder for them, because their child had only been a part of their lives for a short time, so there would be less of a sense of everything being different, and all the accompanying losses that losing someone who has been a part of the family for some time brings.'

They are thoughtful and generous responses, ways of saying to the other parents in the group that their grief was truly understood. The truth, a truth the parents understood in their hearts, is that grief is never quantifiable.

> The enduring pain of losing a child cannot be measured, so it is not possible to say that it is more or less painful to lose a child suddenly or after a long debilitating illness, nor can it be assumed that the age of the child determines the intensity of the emotions. (Hindmarch 2009, pp.5–6)

But the group's conversation raised questions about how parents who only have a short time with their child grow and hold a sustaining internal bond.

Amalia and Avi's daughter Hannah was diagnosed with a diaphragmatic hernia at the 24-week scan. The breach in the diaphragm meant that the developing bowel was pushing up into the chest cavity as Hannah grew in the womb, compromising the growth of her lungs. Whilst she was in her mother's womb she was receiving all the oxygen she required through the umbilical cord. But at birth, when her breathing would normally be taken over by her lungs, she would struggle. At Amalia's antenatal appointments doctors explained that it was highly likely that Hannah would not live for more than a few hours, but like many parents in this situation, her parents continued to hold a hope that their little girl's condition would not be as severe as the scans suggested, and that she would survive. Sadly, their daughter's condition was as serious as predicted; she was put on a ventilator to enable her to breathe at birth but lived for only six days. In her brief life her heartbroken parents kept a constant vigil beside her cot on the neonatal intensive care unit. This was a time for a few close family members to visit and meet Hannah, to say hello and goodbye. Amalia and Avi wanted to record this time in as many ways as they could and took photographs and videos of their little girl. They wrote a diary, supported by the staff on the ward, who added their own thoughts and feelings. In the pictures, Hannah's tiny face is mostly obscured by the tube that was helping her breathe and her feeding tube.

When Hannah's lung collapsed for the third time it was agreed that it was time for Hannah to be relieved of all the tubes, and for her to die in the arms of her mother. This was Amalia's first opportunity to gaze upon her daughter's face no longer obscured by tubes. She could move her freely from arm to arm, and pass her to her husband to hold. After she died Amalia was able to bathe her, change her nappy and dress her for the first time. It was a time for more photographs to be taken.

Amalia visited her little girl whilst she was in the mortuary. In the visiting room, with the support of the mortuary staff, Amalia was able to bathe, dress and hold her little girl twice more. It was here that Amalia was able to be a mother to her baby, privately, away from the busyness of the ward, and also prolong the time she had to nurture and strengthen her bond with her. Throughout she was supported tenderly by her husband, who held Amalia in a way that made it possible for her to hold her first child, in what were the most distressing circumstances.

Chinua had two sons and longed for a daughter. When she became pregnant for a third time and her scan showed she was carrying a daughter, her happiness knew no bounds. She took great pleasure in preparing for her arrival, buying pretty dresses and accessories. Tragically, as a consequence of complications in the delivery, the baby girl was starved of oxygen and died at the age of three days. Chinua was felled by grief.

On the neonatal intensive care ward Chinua cradled her daughter Shona for several hours before carrying her to the mortuary, to leave her in the care of the mortuary staff. Like Amalia, she visited her baby in the mortuary, to hold and bathe her. She decided that all the beautiful clothes she had prepared for her baby were not appropriate for her funeral and, with a friend, made a special journey into London to choose a dress for Shona to wear. She told the staff in the shop the reason she was there, and they helped her with her choice. Dressing her baby for the final time was deeply sad and meaningful. Her husband took photographs of mother and baby.

As Chinua described all she did for her daughter after her death and before her funeral, it was as if time had slowed down during that short period. She carried out everything with great care and deliberation. Sharing her story with strangers meant that others, as well as close friends and family, knew about Shona, and that felt important. It was as if, given the little time together they had, Chinua was unconsciously weaving new threads into her bond with her baby during the brief period between her birth and funeral.

Parents who came for counselling who had lost their child before birth or in the neonatal period attended for no shorter time than those who had had their children with them for longer. Although their time with them on earth had been brief, there was always so much to talk about and so much to grieve. All those I saw for counselling who had been encouraged to spend time with their child after death valued it dearly. There was much to tell about the hours they had spent together, and it wasn't always easy to talk to others about time spent with a child who has died.

Nor can it be easy for parents to know how to be with a baby who has died. It is not something anyone can ever be prepared for. A research study which looked at mothers' experiences of stillbirth and opportunities for memory making found that sometimes mothers had expressed a reluctance to touch and hold their stillborn babies because they were not sure what effect that handling would have (Brierley-Jones *et al.* 2014–2015). Somehow it didn't feel 'right' to hold or take photographs of the baby and some were fearful of how the baby would look or feel to the touch, or that they might hurt their baby. Being in a hospital where there are procedures and regulations made some new mothers concerned about what they were 'allowed' to do. Feeling they were not in control of what was happening was a common experience.

Brenda, the mother of baby Harry who died shortly after birth, told me she was encouraged to hold Harry for the short time before he died. She and her partner were taken to a private, quiet room to be with him, but they felt that because of a concern to give them privacy they were not given enough support and information. They felt embarrassed to ask what they believed were questions they should know the answers to, and were unsure whether they were allowed to put Harry down for a while so they could take a break. They felt they might be judged if they did. They were also worried about not being confident that they would know when he had died.

Getting the balance between support and privacy, allowing parents to feel they are in control and helping them know what to do is a difficult judgement for staff, who may not have known the parents for very long.

Parents from an ethnic minority community may face further challenges because of the expectations of their culture. I recently met two women, one Muslim woman and one Jain woman, who had both had stillborn babies. They described their bewilderment and helplessness, their 'not knowing what to do' because their experience was that in their culture people didn't speak about babies dying. After a death there are a few days of mourning and then there should be acceptance and moving on. But when a baby is stillborn there is no mourning period.

One of the women was second generation and both had adopted a Western lifestyle, but in the distressing and unfamiliar situation of losing a baby before birth they turned to their parents for support and advice. Their parents in turn sought help from their community and their faith leaders. The Muslim mother was told to accept what had happened and to allow the hospital to arrange the funeral. She was determined not to do this and fought hard to give her baby a proper Muslim funeral. Although the Muslim community is tight-knit and supportive, stillbirth can carry a stigma, and often nobody will speak about it. Women may feel they are to blame, and may be told to accept that it is God's will.

Since their loss both women have become supporters of other women with ethnic minority heritage who lose their babies, through the stillbirth and neonatal death charity Sands (see the Resources section at the end of this book), helping to ensure that women in their situation have an alternative place to seek advice. They told me that the women they speak to tend to favour telephone counselling because it is more private and they don't feel so exposed.

In the hospital where I worked we were fortunate to have a Muslim chaplain who was able to provide a supportive and advisory link between bereaved parents and their communities.

Over the last thirty years there have been differing views about how helpful it is for the parents of a stillborn baby to spend time with their infant after the birth. Many mothers and fathers who have done so value it highly, knowing that, for them, it is an essential element of the continuing bond with their baby that began in pregnancy. This is the time when the baby is held both literally and symbolically in the family and incorporated into their biography. However, some research has suggested that mothers who spend time with their stillborn baby are more at risk of depression and anxiety in a future pregnancy and may have problems of attachment to a baby who is born subsequent to the loss (a helpful summary of this is in Brierley-Jones *et al.* 2014–2015, pp.145–146).

Clearly what is best and most helpful depends on what the parents themselves feel they need and are most comfortable in doing at the time. What is unhelpful is the assumption that what is right for one is right for all. Parents need information, choice and support. A more recent research study has shown that it is important for mothers who choose to spend time with their stillborn infants to be given the opportunity to talk about it afterwards. 'It is not the opportunity to make memories per se that affects the future mental health of the mother but whether mothers have the opportunity to share and process these memories afterwards' (Crawley, Lomax and Ayers 2013, cited in Brierley-Jones *et al.* 2014–2015, p.146).

This was something Amalia was able to do in counselling. Amalia showed me the photographs of Hannah. The album was divided into two parts: before she died and afterwards. At the junction of these two parts Amalia had written what she described as a 'warning', so that people could choose whether they wanted to look at the pictures of Hannah after her death. Amalia needed and desired to dwell on every tiny detail of her daughter's life and death. As we looked at the photographs together Amalia pointed out the small but visible changes in Hannah after she had died and as the days passed. She was not uncomfortable with them, but, because she had had so little time with her child, she wanted to take in everything.

Parents who lose a child in the early days lose all the future hopes and plans they had made from the moment the pregnancy was confirmed. For all parents, a bond with their child begins well before birth. The mother throughout the nine months thinks and dreams about the child she is carrying, and imagines what her child will be like. A pregnant woman is highly attuned to the movements and patterns of her unborn child, who is both within and part of her, and sometimes expressed as a deep introspection and self-absorption. An element of that is an anticipation of something coming to an end, and the loss that will bring (for a few women for whom pregnancy is difficult and uncomfortable, a welcome loss perhaps, but a loss nonetheless). When my daughter was nearing the end of her first pregnancy she spoke of an anticipatory sadness about the loss of her exclusive relationship with the baby she was carrying: 'I'm going to have to share her.' She fantasised about taking herself off with her unborn child to an island somewhere, so that they could always be 'just the two of us'.

For all women, and for most fathers, when a baby is born, there is already a relationship in place which has been growing and treasured for many months. For parents whose child is well, pre-birth conjectures about the loss birth brings are eclipsed by the very real presence of a demanding baby. But for parents whose baby dies at or shortly after birth there is both the loss that comes with the ending of pregnancy and no comfort of there now being a baby to hold, only emptiness. For them the prenatal thoughts and dreams are all they have and as such are deeply valued and held. For Chinua, Shona would have been her princess, her beautiful, feminine little girl. These are the bonds that parents draw from in their grief.

For the parents who are never able to take their baby home, the whole of their relationship with their baby will have been lived in a public arena. There will have been no time of total privacy for the parents and the baby, except after the baby has died. And even this will have been in a hospital environment and not in the privacy of home. Perhaps this makes the exclusiveness and intimacy of the pregnancy especially important. It is important though for parents to know that they are able to take their baby home after death, if this is something they would feel comfortable with. The practicalities can be challenging, especially the need for the baby to be kept cool, so when parents do make this choice, they usually only have their baby at home for a short time. However, very recently in some hospitals and hospices refrigerated Moses baskets have been available; called 'cuddle cots', they provide a cool environment for the baby's body and give the parents more time to make memories together.

A moving piece of research in the USA followed thirty parents who chose to continue with a pregnancy when there had been an antenatal diagnosis of a 'lethal condition' (Cote-Arsenault *et al.* 2015). The parents knew that their babies were likely to be stillborn or to only live for a few hours after birth. The study showed that these parents engaged in parenting of their unborn child that was 'deliberate, accelerated and compressed, knowing that their time with their baby was brief' (Cote-Arsenault *et al.* 2015). During the pregnancy and after birth they were highly protective of their baby, making sure the baby was comfortable, warm and not left alone. Parents did all they could to promote the personhood of their baby and the value of their baby's brief life, and ascribed qualities such as a 'fighter' or 'feisty' with pride. Through their interaction with their baby before and after birth, and then spending time together, parents built strong, loving bonds. Sadness came later.

Oliver and Kelly were told at the twelve-week scan of their first baby, Levi, that there were signs of a chromosomal problem. Over the following weeks it was confirmed that he had Trisomy 18 (Edward's syndrome) and that if he lived to full term, his parents would have only a very brief time with him after his birth. Oliver and Kelly are Christians and, shortly before Kelly was due to give birth, they sent out a letter in the form of a prayer guide to their friends and family, sharing how they were feeling and asking for prayer. This moving and courageous letter placed the coming days very firmly in God's hands, and included a tender description of the loving bond they had created with Levi during the pregnancy and to whom they ascribed a very strong personhood.

'...the doctors have told us that with all these complications he was unlikely to make it to full term, but he's defied that and kept going! We're proud of him and we've really enjoyed the time we've had with him, although it has of course been an incredibly hard time.'

Oliver and Kelly were able to spend two precious hours with their baby after he was born and he was able to meet his three grandparents.

When a baby dies the mother is given drugs to suppress her production of milk. But it is not only her breasts that have prepared for the baby; the whole of her body is in a state of preparedness. So the arms that never get to hold the baby, or only hold the baby for a brief time, literally ache with emptiness; the senses that were anticipating the sight, smell and touch of their newborn are unsatisfied; and the whole body experiences physical anguish and yearning. Sadly it is the physicality of the loss that cannot be recreated in the continuing bonds. Parents, especially mothers, search for it through the smells and touch of the blankets and clothes their baby used. But these sensory comforts fade long before the pain of longing begins to ease.

Tragically, parents who lose a baby neonatally rarely have much that is material to treasure and to show to others. As with Amalia and Chinua, there may be photographs that have been taken by parents and family. (There are now, on some neonatal wards, contact details of skilled and sensitive photographers who will come into the hospital and, for no charge, take pictures of the baby with parents after death. At some hospitals there is also an opportunity for parents to have foot and hand imprints, cast into clay, glazed and framed as a memento.) There will be the name band that encircled the baby's wrist in the hospital, possibly a blanket and soft toy that had shared the cot, and cards received, paradoxically both congratulations and sympathy cards. But few people are able to say that they knew the baby, other than hospital staff and immediate family.

As one parent of a baby boy who died just a few hours after birth said, 'I wish more people had met Michael, because then I could talk about him more.' One of the ways we strengthen connections with our children is through our relationships with others who know them. Without these it can sometimes feel like the child was never really ever there.

Chapter 4

HOW A GROUP CAN
STRENGTHEN THE BOND

*'I had you and I have you now no more.' O little words how
can you run so straight across the page, beneath the weight
you bear?*

Edna St Vincent Millay (1892–1950), 'Interim',
in *Renascence and Other Poems* (1917)

One of the services offered to bereaved parents in the
hospital where I worked was an invitation to join a group
a colleague and I facilitated. This invitation was sent to
parents three months after their child had died, recognising
that during the early weeks most are in a state of shock and
unlikely to be able to think clearly about what they might
find helpful, beyond being with close family and friends and
making arrangements for their child's funeral.

For some the arrival of a letter from the hospital was
not welcome, but for most it meant that they were still
being remembered by those who had cared for their child.
Some parents responded immediately that this would be
something they would like to do, whilst others held back
for a while. Others knew that going to a group and meeting
with other bereaved parents would never be something they
wanted to do.

The group met every two months for an hour and a half
and was open-ended, meaning that new members could
join at any time. Parents were welcome to come just the
once, to come regularly or just from time to time. What was

important was that they let me know if they were coming, so that I could have the room ready and welcoming with the right amount of seating, that they arrived on time, and that the group was not interrupted once it had started.

The group was held in the house that provided accommodation for parents whose children were inpatients. Some wards at the hospital provided a camp bed for one parent next to their child's bed, but this was not usually appropriate on the paediatric intensive care ward. When both parents needed accommodation, and sometimes siblings too, and when a child's stay in hospital extended to weeks and months, being able to stay at the Ronald McDonald House was a lifeline. For many parents, returning to the parents' accommodation was an emotional experience, connecting them with the time they were there and their child was alive and an inpatient; for some, this was a treasured connection, whilst for others it was painful. For parents who hadn't stayed in the parents' accommodation, perhaps because they lived locally, or more usually because their child's time in hospital had been brief and they had been able to stay on the ward, or in the few emergency beds attached to the paediatric intensive care unit, it was an unfamiliar environment, albeit with connections to the hospital.

Parents came to the group with many and differing feelings about what it meant to be there, and to what extent the place connected them with their child.

For the group to be accessible to as many parents as possible, a free crèche was provided, funded by the paediatric intensive care ward funds. Some parents who used it were grateful for the opportunity it gave them to come as a couple. All the parents who used it were glad not to have to ask friends or family to care for their children whilst they attended, and valued knowing that their children were physically close by. I wondered how it was for parents who had no other children, and who would be aware of the presence of the crèche in a nearby room, but felt that this was an issue that could be spoken about in the group, and shouldn't get in the way of the provision.

The group always started with each parent sharing the story of their child. If both parents were present there was usually a negotiation between them about who would tell the story on this occasion. Usually one parent would begin and the other would add to the telling. Sometimes the telling of the stories would take up almost all the group time, especially if it was a large group. Frequently the group would give a parent more than their share of the time, perhaps if it was a first time, or if the group judged them to be particularly in need of talking. It was striking how the group would be able to make these kinds of decisions without discussion. It was, I felt, a true measure of how the members of the group were comfortable and in tune with each other.

Parents who had been coming to the group for a while had shared their child's story several times. But on each occasion there were new listeners, and even when there weren't, new elements of their story would emerge with the retelling. The focus might be on what their child was like, their time in hospital, or their experience of their child's death. Invariably this sharing of their child's story was a time of high expressed emotion, not only for the speakers but also for the listeners.

In his classic work on groups, *The Theory and Practice of Group Psychotherapy*, psychotherapist Irvin Yalom (Yalom with Leszcz 2005) identifies a number of therapeutic elements that occur. One is catharsis, which is the feeling of relief that comes from the release of pent-up emotions, such as when a story has been told in a group and the accompanying emotions expressed without holding back. For these bereaved parents telling their story was cathartic, and for those listening there was not only the inherent sadness of the story itself, witnessing the distress of the parents telling it, but also the echoes with their own experience and memories. Parents speaking would feel greatly supported by what they received from the other parents, whether words of support and understanding or simply tears shed.

Yalom writes about the capacity for people in a group to transcend themselves (if only temporarily) through the absorption in another's story (Yalom with Leszcz 2005). Listening to others' stories can offer relief for those who are finding themselves overwhelmingly preoccupied by their own experiences. It is important to remember that the participants in the group were self-selected. The parents who came and continued to come were those who found such group processes resonant with their needs.

Once individual stories were spoken and heard, the group would move to talking more generally about their experiences and thoughts. A recurring focus for the group was a shared view that other people can never truly understand what it is to lose a child, even though they may try very hard. Only those who have experienced it can properly understand, and know how to say the right things and respond in the right way. These beliefs were affirming for the members (though less so for me, the facilitator, who could identify the shared belief but was not a bereaved parent myself), and united the group strongly both through their shared experience and difference from others. Yalom calls this universality: the recognition that shared experiences in a group can help its members feel less isolated and more validated; and this in turn raises members' self-esteem (Yalom with Leszcz 2005).

The belief that only those who had been bereaved of a child could properly understand would be backed up with stories of how others had said or done the wrong things. At the same time there was an agreement that others would not necessarily know any better, and that they might have made the same mistakes themselves before they were bereaved. Parents had similar experiences of what had been unhelpful and, sometimes, hurtful things to hear. These included an opinion about when the parent might begin to feel better or 'get over it', and a view about the possible helpfulness of a future pregnancy. The parents found any suggestion that having other children remaining might be a blessing or a source of comfort very uncomfortable to hear. Many of the parents in the group had lost a child who had been living with an illness or disability, and comments from others who were not bereaved about the quality of the child's life had they lived, or the possibility that death itself could have brought some relief from suffering, were not welcome. (It may be that, at some point in the far-off future and in the quietness of their own hearts, parents might wonder these things. But these were too deep and complex thoughts to be shared in everyday conversation.)

Parents spoke about how they never found it kind or helpful if someone suggested that they understood how they felt because they had been bereaved, not of a child, but of a parent or friend, even a pet, or that they knew someone else who had lost a child.

However, the collective view was always that saying something, even if it was not the most appropriate thing, was better than saying nothing. And crossing the road or ignoring you in the supermarket was possibly the worst thing of all.

Along with the experience of hearing unhelpful things, most parents shared the view that as a bereaved parent they were now subject to others' judgements (often contradictory) about how they should behave: for example, if the loss is of a baby, then it would be a good idea to try for another quite soon, but if an older child dies then a 'decent' period should elapse; it would be a good idea to go and talk to a counsellor, or best not to talk about it too much or you will find yourself dwelling on it; either you need to withdraw from life and grieve privately or better to get out there and get on with life, particularly for the sake of the other children. Parents agreed that they had been surprised to encounter other people's strong and sometimes forceful beliefs about how they, as bereaved parents, should behave.

They also agreed about what they had found to be supportive, and this always included being given an opportunity to speak about their child. They valued being asked questions about them, especially when people were sensitive enough to know just how much to ask without appearing to be vicariously interested. Most parents enjoyed talking about their lives with their child when their child had been well, and through the telling of these stories remembering and feeling close to their child. They also valued others sharing with them something they remembered about their child.

There were times when the group felt confident enough with each other to talk together about some very difficult issues to do with their child's death. For many this was the first time they had experienced being with a dead body, and for all the first time it had been the body of a child, and a child who was their own. In addition they had to find ways of managing all that follows death, the mortuary and possible post-mortem, funeral directors and the funeral. There is a reluctance to talk in much detail about these things even when an adult dies; and how much more so when it is a child. Parents found themselves in an alien and traumatic place at a time when they were at their most vulnerable. Being able to share very similar experiences which others would rarely talk about helped them feel less alone.

The group understood that, for many, speaking about those final days, hours and moments with their child was deeply personal, and not easy. Hearing others speak about them in the group was painful and not easy, particularly when a parent had not been able to be with their child at the end of their life, or unable to spend time with their child after death.

Asha grieved that she had not spent more than an hour with her stillborn child. She had felt weak and exhausted after the birth and had needed to sleep. When she looked back to this time she remembered feeling confused and detached. After her baby had been taken to the mortuary, she didn't see him again. She hadn't known that she was able to, and somehow nobody had told her she could. She felt sad and envious when others spoke of their different experiences, and needed the comfort and reassurance of the group that she had not, in any way, let her child down.

After the death of a child parents have to make difficult decisions in a short time. One that the group would consider was how they decided whether to have their child buried or cremated. For some families this was straightforward as it was determined by their culture or religious beliefs, but for others it was just not something they ever imagined having to think through. Even though by the time it was being discussed in the group parents had already made the choice, it was good to share with others the agonies of that decision. Within the group parents had made different choices, and members were always good at affirming the decisions of others, whatever they had been.

Practical advice and information from other members of the group was more acceptable than when it came from family and friends. The parents were less constrained than I was about giving advice. James and Erica were relieved and liberated when the group told them unanimously that it was okay not to spend Christmas Day with the extended family, where there would be a new baby present.

The group was particularly significant for fathers. As well as being more inhibited showing and talking about their feelings, men also had fewer opportunities. Fathers were more likely to return to work before mothers and consequently find themselves back in the world sooner. Following a neonatal death, mothers will have maternity leave to take, and for mothers of older children, employers are likely to show a compassionate attitude to the timing of a return to work. Many fathers believed that their first responsibility was to support their partner in her grief, and to show themselves strong enough to hold the family together. There were times when I heard mothers say that they wished their partners would not try to be so strong and allow themselves to be more open about their feelings.

Coming to the group and meeting other men there helped fathers feel that they were not alone in their need to talk. Stories of how hard it can be to show emotion were shared, and I was struck that if a man did become tearful in the group, it was usually the other men who reached out to him.

Yalom (Yalom with Leszcz 2005) writes about how imitative behaviour in a group can be therapeutic. For the men attending the group, the presence of other men expressing emotion, and at times weeping openly for their child, was freeing to men who might otherwise feel constrained. Fathers would say that the group was the only place where they were able to do this, and their partners would express relief to see them 'letting go'. At times mothers would express a worry that their partners didn't seem to be grieving much, and that made them upset and wonder whether their partner had loved the child as deeply as they did.

I felt that for some men, and maybe for some women too, talking felt easier in a group than in the intimacy of one-to-one counselling. It was possible to withdraw when speaking became hard and words just wouldn't come, or at the times when it felt awkward. It was also easier in a group to laugh. Some of the most memorable times I had in the group were when we were able to laugh together.

James lost his son Barney when he was eighteen months old. In the group he spoke about how he would be managing his day well, and then would suddenly experience an overwhelming onslaught of grief, which literally would bring him to his knees. As he worked as a roofer the other men in the group, whilst being respectful and sympathetic, also took pleasure in imagining how that might be for James if he were several metres above the ground when this happened, and how his work mates might interpret James being on his knees in the middle of a job.

For many parents, in the darkest times of shock and sorrow, there can be moments which may appear absurd, and when humour is a way of dealing with them. Collecting their child's ashes from the undertaker and then deciding where to keep them until they are scattered carried a crazy unreality which, when discussed in the group, at times led to shared laughter. My sense is that it was only amongst others who have lived through the same experience that this could ever be acceptable.

An issue that united many of the men in the group was how they managed the return to work, sometimes only a short time after the loss of their child. What do you say to your colleagues and work mates? What can you expect from management and bosses? Is it better that everyone knows before you return, or would it be easier to tell people yourself?

Jerry, whose three-month-old baby died of a congenital heart condition, spoke about his wish for colleagues to know what had happened before he returned, but didn't want anyone speaking about it to him at work face to face. He requested this before he returned and his manager made sure his colleagues were told. For Jerry the normality and remoteness of the workplace was a sanctuary to escape to from the sadness at home. He was able to put his grief on hold whilst he was at work.

Andrew, however, wanted his colleagues to speak to him about his daughter Louise, who died when she was eleven. She had been born with complex developmental difficulties which were life limiting, so Andrew's colleagues knew about her and some had met her. It was important that his loss was acknowledged and spoken about, and Andrew found it a comfort to have colleagues checking in with him in the early days after he returned to work, asking him how he was.

In the group difference was heard and understood.

A recurring theme was the fear that memories of the lost child might fade over time: a terror of the possibility of any diminishing of the bond between parent and child. Attending the group and sharing stories helped to strengthen memories and to access new ones. Parents also used the group to share suggestions about what they did to keep memories and the accompanying emotions alive and strong.

Lee lost his only child, Bridie, at the age of two as a consequence of a complex mitochondrial condition. For her first year she had developed normally, and Lee and his wife Sue had taken plenty of videos of her. In the group Lee talked about how afraid he was of losing the intensity of the grief he felt, because he knew that this connected him to his daughter, and that any lessening of this intensity would feel an additional loss. After a day at work Lee would come home and watch videos of his daughter and weep. This assured him that the strong feelings were still there and accessible.

Andy was relieved to hear Lee speak about this in the group. Following the death of his daughter Freya he would often sit in her room at the end of the day, cradle her soft toys and cry. He had felt embarrassed about this because he felt like he was forcing himself to be sad. Lee's story was reassuring, because after time out in the world he had found it helpful to consciously put in place a way to connect again with her loss.

When I took over the group from my predecessor, only one couple stayed on. They had been coming for three years and had become the group's helpful 'grandparents'. They set the style of the group through initiating discussions, sharing photographs of their child and listening attentively. The group had become for them a very important time to devote to remembering and talking about their child. However, once I had settled in as the new facilitator, they made a decision to stop coming, because they felt it was 'time to move on'. Parents who were now coming had only known me as facilitator and the dynamics were changing. Perhaps for this longstanding couple the connection with their child the group had offered might have been challenged by change, and they needed to preserve what was familiar.

As well as being helpful to a new facilitator, longstanding group members are also helpful to the newer group members. When sharing their story they show that the pain of loss does not diminish. But they are living their lives, still together, working, taking holidays, and making friends and plans for the future. They offer what Yalom called the instillation of hope (Yalom with Leszcz 2005). Despite the fears more newly bereaved parents might express, they continue to have a meaningful and strong bond with their child.

Chapter 5

BEGINNING THE TRANSITION: SPIRITUAL MEANINGS AND THE CONTINUING BOND

What is the truth, the eternal truth, of what happened in that shattering moment? As far as our senses can inform us, at one instant there was a body, 'lusty, young and cheerily drawing breath'; alive to the finger tips, intensely conscious of every delight and pain, fair tenement of a most fair spirit, a little brain teeming with plans for her own enjoyment and everyone else's round her. And then a white stillness, utterly unconscious, unspeakably lovely, but – empty. Unfitted to be used any more by the life – all love and joy – which had used it with such love and grace and purpose. That is all our senses could apprehend.

> Eleanor Acland, *Ellen Acland: The Story of a Joyful Life* (1925), written by Lady Acland, following the death of her little daughter on her bicycle

When Jackie's four-month-old baby Charlie died unexpectedly in Accident and Emergency, Jackie and her husband Adam were left in a private room with him so that they could spend time holding him and saying goodbye. The sister in charge suggested that when they were ready to go they should place Charlie in the Moses basket in the room and leave, and that she would then look after him. But for Jackie, this just felt wrong: 'You don't leave your baby in a strange place and walk away. You hand your baby to a person.' More than that, the Moses basket was on the floor, not on a stand. 'Putting him in a basket on the floor had connotations of treating him like an animal – a pet that lives in a basket. Much loved perhaps, but an animal nonetheless.' Jackie needed to entrust Charlie to a person who would hold him; he was a precious child and nothing less. The sister understood, and when Jackie and Adam were ready to leave, they called her and she gently took Charlie into her arms.

When a child dies one of the first things parents have to do is to make a terrible transition: they now have to leave their precious child in a place that is usually an institution and in the care of strangers. This is a child for whom only hours previously they had absolute responsibility and would never dream of letting out of sight unless it was with someone they knew and trusted. To adjust from being in relationship with a living dependent child to a relationship with a child who has died, and no longer has physical and emotional needs, takes more time than circumstances allow and minds can comprehend. So there is this transition period when parents are often very concerned that their child is properly cared for, even though they know logically that their child is no longer a sentient being.

Sometimes the transition is helped by the parents being part of the journey from the ward or the Accident and Emergency department to the mortuary, although for some this is unbearable, and they choose not to be. Parents found that when they met mortuary staff they were touched by their sensitivity and kindness. Their child would be received as if she were still living, and the mortuary staff would promise to take care of her. One mother, who wanted to visit her baby in the mortuary, was concerned that her baby might not smell the same when she returned. A member of the mortuary staff suggested that she brought in a bottle of the baby bath product she used so that they could bath the baby in this when the mother came.

For parents whose children die in a hospice the transition is made easier by the provision of a cool room where children can be looked after from when they die until their funeral, or until they are transferred to the care of a funeral director. Here the family can spend as much time with their child as they want. Other family members and friends can also come and say goodbye and offer support.

The psychoanalyst John Bowlby, in his work on attachment, wrote that in the early stage after death the newly bereaved are not able to fully register the permanence of the separation from their loved one (Bowlby 1980). This is because our separation response is generated by a more primitive part of the brain, and it is only when the more evolved parts of the brain come into play that we can begin to comprehend that a person is lost forever. And so there is this intermediate state when physical proximity to the child is still very important, and its absence feels utterly wrong.

For parents it can be inconceivable to imagine their child in a mortuary because the child still has a very real physicality. And so it only feels right to know that their child will be placed in the mortuary in a fridge with other children and not adults. Some children's hospitals have their own mortuary which is separate from the adult mortuary.

Similarly, parents who have their child buried will often express relief that their child is in an area of the cemetery or churchyard specifically designated for children. Parents who decide to have their child cremated may choose to keep the ashes because it is comforting to hold onto a physical remnant of their child's physical being. Some will incorporate some of the ashes into a pendant that can be worn. When parents bury their child or scatter their ashes, proximity to the family home can be an important consideration. Scattering ashes around a tree which is grown in a pot means that if the family move away, they can be taken with them.

Adele and Martin took the opportunity to travel shortly after the unexpected death of their only child Tabitha. Family and friends encouraged them to 'get away and put it all behind them'. This was, of course, impossible, as thoughts and memories of Tabitha travelled with them. But what they unexpectedly found unbearable was the geographical distance between them and where she was buried. In these early months they needed to be close to her, and so they returned home.

The transition from a relationship with a living being to one who has died is the first step in the move towards the creation of a new, changed bond with the child. Perhaps it is through this painful, slow letting go that something else can begin to grow. But it takes time.

I think for parents who know their child will die, and when the child knows too, this transition can begin before death. Parents of children who are dying sometimes described what they saw as 'otherworldliness' in the way their child related to them and others. They would sometimes speak about it in terms of the child 'drawing others to themselves'. It may be that as the confines of our outer world increase the inner world grows brighter.

Parents described what they saw to be special qualities their child possessed, which made them different from other children. If their child had endured a prolonged illness or had been living with a disability, they would often be attributed exceptional attributes like patience, kindness, strength and wisdom. They might also be described as possessing a capacity for knowing and perception that was beyond their years. Likewise, children who died who did not have a pre-existing disability or illness were, retrospectively, perceived to have possessed qualities that had made them special or different. Parents would speak of their child as 'too good for this world' or that God 'needed another angel'.

Monica and John had five children. Their eldest, Juan, was seriously disabled with cerebral palsy. As he grew older he developed problems with his lungs and had repeated chest infections. As his twelfth birthday approached he asked for a special party for his family and friends. This was a surprising request because Juan was a shy boy who usually found large social gatherings challenging. But he was insistent and his parents honoured his request. The party was a great success and Juan loved every moment. Two weeks later he developed a severe chest infection which ended his life. His parents believed Juan knew that he was nearing the end of his life and had wanted to say goodbye to everyone.

Did Juan's wish for a party come from knowing that he was nearing the end of his life? The possibility of this was a comfort to his parents. They had always seen Juan as possessing a special gift of perception even though he spoke only a few words.

When Bridie died her parents, Lee and Sue, decided to have her buried. For Sue, visiting Bridie's grave every day became an essential part of her life, and she would talk to her daughter about how sad she was feeling and how much she missed her. Two years on and Lee and Sue began to consider having another child. But this decision could not be made without Bridie's endorsement and Sue would speak about this to her daughter at the grave. When Sue became pregnant, she believed that Bridie was now ready for this to happen.

However unusual Sue's behaviour might appear, what this couple did was bring Bridie right into their planning for the future. Bridie became part of this next step, and in that way Sue and Lee were strengthening their bond with their first child. What these parents found helpful was to ascribe to their daughter powers that are not unlike those that are ascribed to an oracle.

The belief that their child's presence and influence did not end with death was common amongst the parents I met, irrespective of their religious faith. Those with a religious faith were able to draw on their faith's teaching as to the nature and form that afterlife took, but for those without I was struck that there appeared to be commonly recurring themes.

In our imaginings the death of a child belongs to a world where things have gone badly wrong. It is the nightmare end to the fairy stories we grew up with. Sleeping Beauty is not awakened from her slumber by a kiss, Snow White is poisoned by the apple and remains in her grave, Hansel and Gretel are murdered by the wicked witch, and Red Riding Hood is devoured by the wolf. Deep in our psyche concepts of illness, disability and tragic accidents can be challenged and disrupted by ideas of curses and magic. From her experience of working on a neonatal ward, psychotherapist Margaret Cohen writes that 'the death of a baby is such a dreadful thing that the veneer is ripped away and we are confronted by terrifying thoughts' (Cohen 2003, p.129).

Such strong and strange associations can be most disturbing, especially in the days just after a child has died, and bring distressing feelings of anger, blame and guilt. For parents to manage and survive these dark thoughts, and for them not to disrupt the bond with their child, it is perhaps more than helpful, and indeed it is critical for them, whatever their faith or belief system, to know that their child is now in a safe place, even if that place is simply somewhere the child is no longer suffering.

Bereaved parents may hold a view that their child is now reunited with family members who have died, and that they will be receiving ongoing parenting from them. It is comforting to know that family members are able to continue the care that parents can no longer give: 'I know my dad is up there keeping an eye on him'; 'She's having a cuddle with her grandma.'

Sometimes it is a need for companionship that forms part of parents' understanding of why their child has died. When Angela tragically lost a second child she felt very strongly that her older child had been asking for a playmate and her second child had responded to that calling.

Angels are seen both as guardians of the child who has died and also as the child herself. Sometimes a child's grave will have a statue of an angel or the wording on the headstone will refer to angels, either as guardians or as the child: 'An angel crept down from heaven and took my baby'; 'God wanted another angel and chose my child'; 'Later that evening as we said goodbye, he grew his angel wings.' The lack of clarity about whether the child is an angel or is being cared for by angels does not seem contradictory; for bereaved parents it can be both...and...

Sociologist Tony Walter writes interestingly about this ambiguity and also about how the association of angels with child death (also with some adult death) has recently grown in popularity (Walter 2011). He makes the point that neither in Christian/Judaeo nor Islamic theology do angels have a human origin. They are singularly heavenly bodies that originate from God. However, the idea that a dead child could assume an angelic form has a long history, 'going back to at least the Renaissance and the Baroque in which it became fashionable to picture heavenly winged beings as babies' (Walter 2016, p.8).

Walter suggests that what is helpful about this to the mourner is that it is easier to form a continuing bond with an angel than with a soul. We hold pictures of angels in our minds; an angel is purposeful and is associated with goodness, whilst souls have no form and no agency. Their relationship is with God and not with human beings. Walter writes that 'constructing the dead as an angel allows love to be two ways, flowing from as well as to the deceased' (Walter 2011, p.48).

For some parents, especially in the early days following their loss, there is solace in imagining that not only are they continuing in relationship with their child, but also their child is still seeking them out and is actively present in their world. As an angel the child can be pictured by their parents: a child who is still recognisable but who now has wings which suggest freedom and playfulness. An angel represents goodness, purity and immortality, light and positivity (Walter 2016).

Walter also refers to a study by researcher Helen Keane (2009) which looked at the helpfulness to women who have miscarried of using online memorial sites to share their distress. Through representations of the lost foetus/baby as an angel together with antenatal scan images, the baby who has died has a physical form which can be imagined and related to (Walter 2011).

Despite this society becoming more multifaith and less dogma based, the one Christian story most people know is the nativity, the birth of Christ. It is a story that contains a multitude of angels, announcing the incarnation of Christ to his parents and informing shepherds of the arrival of the promised Messiah. The association of birth with angelic voices is one most of us carry. When a child dies before birth or shortly after, perhaps the heavenly choir feels close at hand.

But I found that as time passed parents tended not to speak much about their child being an angel. I am not sure how enduring the image of the lost child as an angel is, except perhaps on social media. Perhaps as the process of internalising the lost child feels more settled, parents have less need of an external visual representation. Referring to their child as an angel seemed to be mostly only significant in terms of reminding others.

Pete and Jo would always include a sticker of an angel on the greetings cards they sent to friends and family. They felt that it reminded them that their first daughter remained very much part of their family, and they continued to hold her in mind. I don't think they any longer imagined her as an angel; the angel had become a way of representing her.

When Verity finished her counselling with me she gave me a gift. It was a beautiful carved wooden angel. In our work together Verity had occasionally referred to her daughter Maisie, who had died shortly after birth, as an angel, but the angel Verity gave me was an adult. I wondered if the angel represented Maisie now grown and fledged or if she was Maisie's guardian angel. The angel carried a tiny board on which was written 'thank you'. Clearly Verity was wanting to thank me, but because of all the many threads of communication that were there, I wondered too if this gift symbolised Maisie thanking me for looking after her mother, and if I had been perceived as Verity's guardian angel, for a while.

As well as angels, parents would also speak about the significance of such things as stars, butterflies, rainbows and white feathers. These symbols didn't always specifically represent their children but symbolised a link with or communication with them. I was struck by the commonality of these symbols, as if there are shared archetypal meanings.

Stars are always present in our night sky. Even when obscured by clouds we know that they are there. They represent constancy, light, brilliance and beauty. They are where we hang our wishes, hopes and dreams. They can be a beacon of guidance and hope on a dark night. The five-pointed star is a central image in the Christian nativity story, guiding sages and coming to rest over the Messiah. The six-pointed star, the hexagram, can be dated back to the eleventh century as a mystical symbol in Judaism. Over the centuries astrologers have used the stars as ways of interpreting the past and predicting the future. Although stars may be dying, they hold a promise of eternity and travel with us wherever we go. Their light is not a reflected light, but generated from within.

Whilst stars seem to symbolise strong themes of continuity and divinity, butterflies and dragonflies conversely suggest frailty. It may be that for parents they represent the life they perceive their child had; brief yet full of wonder and beauty, the larva having been transformed into great loveliness, if only fleetingly.

And rainbows? Perhaps too it is both their beauty and their impermanence. Even as you watch, they can fade away. In religion and in mythology rainbows represent a promise: a divine oath of no more catastrophes, a promise that the earth will no longer be destroyed. And perhaps for some the rainbow has an ending where there is a better place, where hopes and dreams can be realised.

A white feather is a symbol of peace, and for some parents can suggest a communication from their child, often a message of love.

Anya and Tim were wondering about trying for a child eighteen months after the loss of Benji. Sitting outside together one evening, talking this through, a white feather appeared at their feet. They felt sure this was a communication from Benji that all was well and that they should go ahead.

Stuart spoke about 'looking for signs' after his son Toby died. These were not visible signs but interventions. He found that he would ask for his help if he was faced with a difficulty or had lost something, and when things turned out right or he found what he had lost, he would say to himself that it was only a coincidence, but 'inside I know that Toby is there helping me'.

Perhaps for those who have not lost a child, and maybe for some who have, such symbols and their interpretation can appear strange and fanciful. But what I found deeply moving was that when parents shared these beliefs with others in the group, they were always heard with respect and understanding.

Some parents used symbols as a way of incorporating their child in communications such as greeting cards. When it doesn't feel appropriate to include the child's name, a hand-drawn star or rainbow sticker shows that their lost child continued as an integral part of the family.

For many who are bereaved, whether the loss is an adult or a child, a lighted candle holds powerful symbolism. Parents will often choose to light a candle on a significant birthday or on the anniversary of the loss.

After their son died Juliet and her partner Mark could not let his birthday pass without baking a cake. They resolved the question of how many candles by only ever having one. Their other children joined in the making, decorating and eating of the cake, and in blowing out the candle – rituals that were familiar and easily understood, although the extinguished candle held a deeper meaning for Juliet and Mark.

At the Time to Remember services parents receive a lighted candle, which for many is the high point in the act of remembering. As the name of every child is read aloud, each is represented by a single flame. Amongst the parents present there is a strong sense of unity and solidarity. There is also a truly terrible realisation that 'all these children have died'. Parents would light the candles again at home to bring back that feeling of togetherness.

What is it about a lighted candle that holds such meaning? In Jewish and Christian traditions lighting candles dates back to the Hebrews who were told by God to light the temple with lamps to represent God's presence amongst His people. In later Christian theology, a lighted candle represents the light of Christ, dispelling the darkness and bringing hope. For Jews the Menorah candles, celebrating Hanukkah, the Festival of Lights, symbolise God's blessing.

In Hinduism at Diwali, the Festival of Lights, the candle represents the victory of light over dark.

For people of many faiths, and I am sure for people of none, the lighted candle is a symbol which has a shared, though not always articulated, meaning. It is to do with the triumph of good over bad, and hope over despair. Lighting a candle is a purposeful and good act which unites parents both with each other and with their own and each other's children.

When a child dies their possessions can acquire a symbolic meaning, so the handling of them can become highly sensitive and laden with meaning. When there are other children in the family parents may set aside one or two of the toys their child was especially attached to, which are not then available for siblings to play with. Similarly with clothes, some are especially chosen to be kept apart, whilst others may be handed down or given away. Occasionally everything that was part of a child's material world is too precious to pass on or even touch for a while.

Julia and Trevor's only daughter Mia died of a heart condition when she was three. After her death her distraught parents were unable to touch or move anything in her room; it remained as it was when she was alive. Three years later Julia became pregnant, and Mia's room was going to be needed for the baby. It was only then that these parents were able to slowly and painfully sort through Mia's room and decide what to save as hers alone, what to pass on to their next child and what to let go of completely. Family and friends had been very concerned about this couple's decision to leave Mia's room untouched for so long, but for Julia and Trevor, this timing was what they found easiest, and that was all that mattered.

During her pregnancy, Chinua had gathered together a wardrobe of beautiful clothes for her first daughter, Shona, who died at birth. After Shona died Chinua held on to the clothes in the hope that she would conceive again, but as the months and then years passed she had to accept that this was unlikely. Giving away these beautiful dresses to pregnant friends and women in her neighbourhood, not all at once but over time, helped Chinua to gradually and gently let go of her hope for a daughter. Shona would always be her only daughter, but her future had only been imagined. Letting go of her clothes was a way of letting go of this imagined future.

The timing of letting go of a child's clothes and possessions is a very personal decision and it can be especially difficult if parents are not in agreement about it. As we saw with Julia and Trevor, for some it can take years. There are no absolutes about when is best for any parents, though friends and family often express a view about it which is rarely helpful.

When Darren and Kerry's daughter died after several months in hospital, their friends, at their request, came to their home and put away everything that had been part of the child's life: her cot, her toys, her clothes. After some days staying with family, Darren and Kerry returned home and were helped by not having to face reminders of their child there. This was what worked best for them. They grieved their child deeply, but knew that being exposed to physical reminders of her would be overwhelming.

Seven years after the death of her only child Natalie, Kate had put away everything that had belonged to her apart from her wellington boots, which were to always stay by the front door.

The older a child is at the time of their death, the more likely it is that there will be more physical reminders in the home. Siblings may become involved in decisions about what is kept, and create their own memory box to hold precious things that will always connect them with their brother or sister.

When babies die at birth or in the first days, and have never been taken home, parents can feel sad that there is so little that carries their imprint. There may have been a cot, clothes and toys, but these have not been used. It can feel terribly sad that so few people had known their child. Remembering a child is so often enhanced by others' experiences of that child, and when the loss is early, parents have only their own memories to draw on. It is then that staff on the neonatal wards can become very significant because they did know the child, if only fleetingly, and provided care. On some neonatal wards nursing staff write diaries for parents, recounting the minutiae of each day of the baby's life. For parents, these become treasured records not only of a brief life, but also of the people who knew their child.

Chapter 6

THE PLACE OF RITUAL IN MAINTAINING AND NOURISHING THE BOND

Back when I believed in luck, when I was a wisher on stars and white horses and pennies dropped in fountains.

Elizabeth McCracken, *An Exact Replica of a Figment of My Imagination* (2009)

When a child dies, even when the death has been expected, parents' immediate emotions are of shock, fear and bewilderment. Many would say that everything around them feels unreal; it is like they are dreaming. It can be very difficult to know what to do, who to be with and how to speak. Some parents want to leave the hospital and get home as quickly as possible, others find the thought of walking away from their child unbearable. Some find it easier to surround themselves with friends and family, others want to be alone or simply with their partner. As these early days often continue to feel unreal and formless, for many parents planning a funeral offers some temporary relief. It brings tasks which have a structure and order, and people around to advise and guide.

In the words of Jasmine's mother Penny:

Immediately after Jasmine died Tony and I didn't know what to do with ourselves. Up until then all we had thought about was being with Jasmine, and then suddenly she no longer needed us to be there. Having to plan her funeral was a relief in a way. It was a distraction and gave us something that we could still do for her. It was something we could talk about to each other and to other people that felt safe.

Most people are familiar with what happens at funerals, and those who have never been to a funeral will probably have read about or watched one on television. However sombre and sad they are, they provide familiar ground in what has become an unfamiliar world. The people who arrange and manage funerals, funeral directors and faith leaders or celebrants, know what they are doing, and convey a gentle reassuring confidence and authority. For parents of some faiths the guidance around what should be said, who should attend and whether the child is buried or cremated is clear and prescribed. But for others these are difficult decisions to make in what can feel like a short period of time.

This is a time when parents can feel that their responsibility for the physical care of their child is not yet finished. Their child's body is no longer with them, but the decisions about what should happen to the body are still very significant. A parent's decision to visit their child in the mortuary or the chapel of rest is not only to do with a need to see and touch their child, but can also be about needing to know that their child is still well cared for. Sometimes it is to be reassured that the child is dressed in warm clothes. At the funeral a father's decision to carry his child's coffin is one of the last acts of physical care for his child.

Deciding what they wish to happen to the body after the funeral is one of the final decisions parents make about their child's physical being. When parents choose to have their child buried there are decisions to be made before the funeral about where they want the grave to be. If they choose cremation, then they have time after the funeral to think about where to place or scatter the ashes.

The funeral is the socially recognised public arena where parents show their grief to others, to just a few close friends and family or to a larger community. And as parents publically mourn their child they demonstrate that although their relationship with their child has been devastatingly disrupted it remains central and all-consuming. At the funeral it is acceptable and expected for parents to talk about the child they grieve; something most of them welcome. It may be the only time they feel they have licence to do so quite so freely. Afterwards they may fear that others find their expressions of grief and conversations too upsetting.

After the funeral parents will treasure the memories of the words spoken and the cards received, and recalling the funeral can be comforting rather than distressing. Given how difficult the period immediately after the death of a child is, even if the death was expected, I was always impressed by how each parent I met had created a funeral they felt proud of, which spoke to their hearts and which honoured their child.

However, for many families it is the period immediately following the funeral that is very difficult. People who have been supporting them resume their own lives, and some parents have to make decisions about their return to work. Contact with the hospital and all those who have been involved in caring for their child ends, and there is a large space left which had once been filled by the demands of a child. Other children in the family will need to resume familiar routines, and parents have to face the school playground and the supermarket.

Into this emptiness parents begin to create ways of marking the days and months that have passed since their child was with them, in the hope that these rituals will help them feel that their child is very much a part of their everyday lives. In the early months it is usually the day of the month the child died that is remembered and marked, but as time passes this can stretch to the yearly anniversary of the day. But the year holds other significant days: the anniversary of the funeral, the birthday, Mother's Day and Father's Day, the first Christmas. Parents often approach these days with dread, but sometimes find that they are surprised that the anticipated difficult days turn out to be easier than expected. But then, out of the blue, there is a day or a moment – perhaps the first day of term, the glimpse of a newborn baby or the first sighting of daffodils in the park – and a parent is floored by grief.

After their first child, Robin, died shortly after birth, Ellen and Samuel would mark each Thursday, the day he died, by lighting a candle at the end of the day. As time passed they would light a candle on the day of the month he died. When it came to the second anniversary of the day Ellen had learned she was pregnant with Robin, the couple returned to Derbyshire where they had the positive pregnancy test whilst on holiday. They went to a high place and shared a picnic. It felt important that this anniversary was remembered with a celebration. For this couple, building into their lives regular rituals when they remembered Robin together was helpful both in managing the way they shared their grief with each other and keeping them close to their baby son.

When a child is cremated there follows the decision about where to scatter the ashes. Sometimes collecting the ashes and then knowing what to do with them before they are scattered can be difficult. Brenda found herself dreading this. Collecting ashes from funeral directors was not something she had done before, and she didn't know how they would be given to her and how she would be able to face carrying them home. She wondered if she would be allowed to carry them on a bus. She had been told they would be in an urn, but she couldn't picture what that would look like, and whether it would be disrespectful to place the urn in a bag to conceal it. She imagined that when the time came to scatter them there would be very few, because her baby had been so small. Her friend spoke to the funeral directors on her behalf, and found that the concerns Brenda had were not at all unusual. How is anyone expected to know these things? Brenda collected the ashes with her friend, placed the urn in a large handbag which she held closely to her chest, caught the bus home and placed the urn in what she had planned to be her baby's nursery. A few days later she buried some in a pot in which she planted a small tree. She was comforted to know that there were enough to represent a life that had true significance. She also knew that when she moved, the pot and tree could come with her.

Julie and Philip decided to plant a tree in memory of their youngest daughter, Zoe, in their local park. They scattered her ashes beneath it, although they were not sure whether they were allowed to do this. The tree was small and vulnerable in its first year, rather like Zoe, but unlike her, it grew bigger and stronger as the months passed. In its first year her parents worried that it might not survive, and they would have to go through what they were afraid would be a further significant loss. But the tree did well and it came to represent hope. As the seasons changed and the tree blossomed, grew new leaves and then shed them, Julie and Philip were reassured by what represented to them an ongoing cycle of loss and restoration. Julie wrote to me:

> As time has gone on I've come to see how apt the tree is in expressing Zoe's life. The stage before it flowers seems endless each year – the buds are there, almost ready, for weeks. Then it flowers riotously, gloriously for a few days. Then each year, after an agonisingly short time – usually barely a week – the spring winds strip it of its blossom and it's gone for another year.

Their two older children understand what the tree means. They have a place where they can remember their sister in an environment which is associated with play and fun.

Agnes created a small area within the family garden where she sprinkled her daughter's ashes. It was beside her older sons' trampoline, their favourite place. This was where they played and would retreat to when they were feeling quiet or sad.

Parents who decide to have their child buried usually choose a place which they can easily visit, and where they can feel close to their child. Some speak about it in terms of a place 'to spend time with my child', visiting the grave to speak with their child or leave gifts. I doubt any parent who leaves a gift at their child's grave imagines their child would physically engage with it. Nonetheless this can be a symbolic way for parents to continue giving to their child, and brings great comfort.

Nicky and Jim would visit the grave of their daughter Layla, who died when she was three, most weeks in the first year after her death. As time went by they went less frequently, but always at Christmas and on her birthday. On these special occasions they would bring Layla's two sisters, one who was two years older than Layla and the other a year younger. Both sisters would bring a gift to leave. The girls selected the gifts carefully, and in the choosing and the respectful placing of them on the grave Nicky and Jim would find opportunities to talk to them about Layla and their memories of her. The girls never appeared to have a problem deciding what gifts to give. Even though they grew older they continued to choose toys appropriate for a three-year-old. It seemed that they were able to grasp that whilst time moved on for them Layla would never be more than three.

Edward and Rachel found it difficult to decide on the words they wanted inscribed on their son's headstone. They hoped to capture in a few words the kind of child he was, without sounding trite or sentimental. They wanted him to be remembered without pathos. As the months passed it seemed almost impossible for this couple to make a decision, until they realised that their indecision was more to do with a part of them that just could not fully accept that their child had died. They were not ready to set that reality in stone.

Online memorial sites, often linked to websites offering advice and support to bereaved parents or about a particular illness or disability, give bereaved parents the chance to tell their child's story to a limitless and mostly unknown community. Many readers will have experienced a similar loss and some of them will respond to the posting. Over time parents can add to the story and update their memories, but they can also remove those they no longer wish to share.

Just as the bond with the child who has died changes as time passes, though always continues, so too grieving is not static and what feels important can change. When Alice and Mark moved away from the small village where their daughter was buried in the churchyard, they found returning to visit her grave no longer helpful. They felt that she had travelled with them to their new home and was part of family life there. They now remembered her with home-centred rituals and photographs. It was difficult at first not to return regularly to the grave; they felt guilty because it began to look less cared for. But they understood that what was now important for them was to find ways of continuing to remember their daughter that fitted their new lives, and felt meaningful to their other children.

Denise Turner writes about a memorial bench which was bought at the time of her son Joe's death with money raised by local parents (Turner 2014b). A year after his death Denise and her two children, Joe's twin brother Dan and their older sister Amy, marked the anniversary with a ceremony at the bench and released balloons. This became an annual ritual, but as time passed, although it continued to feel important to Amy, Denise felt differently. There was something about the static nature of the bench that no longer reflected how she felt, and visiting it became uncomfortable. The location stopped feeling relevant to Joe's life, and Denise would find herself avoiding it, especially when with others, because she felt she couldn't ignore it, but didn't always want to respond to it. She writes that the permanence of a memorial does not necessarily match the fluid and changing nature of grief, and suggests that more thought needs to be given to help people manage their discomfort when memorials stop feeling appropriate, and support given to families who need to detach from them without feeling guilty.

Rituals and memorials can change as the years go by but parents don't forget. In the early days family and friends remembering the anniversaries and making contact at these times is very important, but after a while inevitably this happens less. Some parents find this hurtful, others less so. One couple told me that in a way they welcomed the forgetting: 'When the family don't remember, Bryony becomes even more our own.'

Chapter 7

HOLDING ON TO THE BOND WHEN ANOTHER CHILD IS BORN

With his birth I have become a father to a living child and a spirit – one child on this side of the curtain and another whispering from behind it.

Jayson Greene, writing in *The Sunday Times*
following the birth of his second child

Something my counselling colleague and I became aware of in our work with bereaved mothers was that the work always intensified if they became pregnant. I learned that when a bereaved mother told me that she was expecting a baby, although my heart might leap, she would be experiencing complex and conflicting emotions. So to simply respond with 'How are you feeling about that?' would be enough. It was likely that she would have already had to field the delight and excitement of family and friends, who would be expecting her to feel the same.

Jill, whose first child Grace died shortly after birth, spoke of her strong reaction, once pregnant again, to the word 'now'. She felt that this small word, spoken by many, both captured everything other people hoped for but dismissed everything that had gone before: 'Now you are going to have a baby that will take your mind off things' (…but I don't want my mind taken off things… I want to remember. Why should now make a difference?); 'Now you are going to have a baby to keep you busy' (…but I still want Grace to keep me busy. Why should that change now?).

For Jill the word 'now' produced an imagined dividing line between the past with Grace and the future with the baby she was carrying, which she didn't recognise or want.

When a woman becomes pregnant not long after the loss of a child, especially if the child has died shortly after birth, she can feel disturbed by the presence of another baby in the place where she had nurtured and grown her lost child. For some women this new baby can feel like a usurper. And whilst previously the first scans, the first flutters of movement and the gradual rounding of her abdomen were perceived with pleasure and joy, this time they may be powerful reminders of the child who grew and moved but no longer lives. At the same time the pregnant mother is also likely to be feeling anxious about whether this pregnancy will end with the birth of a healthy child.

Professor Cote-Arsenault has extensively researched pregnancy following perinatal loss and, drawing from that and her work as a specialist nurse with parents who have suffered the loss of a baby, writes that 'the decision to become pregnant again after loss is not a carefree undertaking. In fact anxiety, depression and fear of attachment are prime characteristics after perinatal loss' (Cote-Arsenault and O'Leary 2015, p.163).

Such pregnancy-specific anxiety tends to fluctuate between scan and antenatal appointments, with mothers feeling more anxious as they approach an appointment, and then reassured when they see or hear the baby, followed by anxiety creeping up again in the days ahead. Anxiety, understandably, tends to be especially high around the time of their previous loss. These mothers become acutely aware of foetal movement, which can be protective, in that they will seek help if there is a diminution, but also preoccupying. Fathers who have lost a baby tend to be more engaged with the pregnant mother than first-time fathers, and pay more attention to the unborn baby's behaviour and presence.

When Rebecca became pregnant three months after the loss of her first child at six days, she spoke of her sadness of what she felt was a loss of innocence. In her first pregnancy she had felt secure and happy. She didn't believe that anything could go wrong. This time she not only felt anxious, but somehow more world-weary and wise. She could not allow herself any glimmers of happiness.

This is a double burden, because not only does the mother hold ongoing sadness but she may also carry guilt. Pregnant women today are aware of the effects of anxiety and depression on the developing baby: that hormones produced when we are anxious and distressed have been found to cross the placenta. The grieving pregnant mother is placed in a situation where she finds herself grieving her lost child and then feeling guilty, because she is afraid her grief may be damaging to her unborn child.

Rebecca developed a strong bond with her first baby, Clare, from early in the pregnancy. She had a difficult relationship with her own mother, whom she experienced as cold and uninterested in her as she was growing up. By the time Rebecca married she was living in a different country from her mother and had little contact with her. She had wanted her own child from a young age, someone she could love unconditionally and begin to repair some of the sadness her own experience of being mothered had left her with. She became pregnant shortly after she married her partner James and everything began to feel right. Like many mothers she took care in the early weeks of her pregnancy to eat and rest properly, and she began talking and singing to her baby. However, a scan at fifteen weeks showed that Clare had a congenital abnormality of the lungs.

It was not possible at that stage for obstetricians to know how badly Clare would be affected, but Rebecca and James were told that there was a possibility Clare might not live after her birth. Rebecca took this in but was concerned that for Clare to do well she should not become too distressed and anxious, so she and James made a very deliberate decision to, as far as possible, put their anxieties on hold. Rebecca continued to enjoy her pregnancy; it felt to her that whilst Clare was in her womb, and not needing to use her lungs to breathe, she was totally safe. She and James prepared for Clare to come home after her birth.

Rebecca's close bond with her daughter was strengthened by seeing her on the regular scans that were required to monitor her development. Clare was born by Caesarean section at thirty-eight weeks. Sadly her lungs were not strong enough and she died at three days.

Although Rebecca met and held her daughter over those three days, she knew that the most significant and important period of her relationship with her daughter had been when she was in the womb. This was when she felt like a proper mother. After her birth Clare's care had to be shared with medical staff, and Rebecca knew that she no longer had control over what happened to her child. Clare left a powerful biological imprint on Rebecca's body, and in the first weeks she grieved physically as well as emotionally. She experienced a deep physical ache in her womb, and when she spoke about her daughter she held her body as if the baby were still there.

Three months after Clare was born Rebecca became pregnant again. This time an early scan showed that the baby was developing normally. Rebecca and James were happy, but for Rebecca especially the happiness was bittersweet. As this baby grew inside her she re-experienced the familiar sensations of her first pregnancy, and these were distressing reminders of the little girl she had loved and lost so early.

It felt harder to love this baby who was in the place where Clare had once been, and yet wasn't Clare; at times it felt as if this baby had 'pushed Clare out'. It was harder too to be excited about this baby because, when she was feeling especially sad, Rebecca admitted that she didn't want this baby, she just wanted Clare.

Having a pregnancy soon after the loss of her baby meant for Rebecca that the precious memories of her pregnancy with Clare, and the strong bonds she formed during that time, became disrupted by the presence of another baby. After the new baby was born, a second little girl she and James called Freya, Rebecca struggled for a while with ambivalent feelings towards her: happy and relieved that she was well and strong but sad and at times angry that she wasn't Clare. Talking through these complicated feelings in counselling, and with the support of James, as the weeks passed Rebecca's bond with Freya strengthened and became less complicated, until she found she could enjoy being a mother to Freya whilst valuing and nurturing her ongoing bond with Clare.

So the arrival of a healthy, lively baby following the loss of a vulnerable sick baby can elicit powerful and conflicting emotions. For one mother it was the very fact that this healthy baby was so strong, so vibrant and so full of life that made her attachment to the frail tiny baby she had lost all the more tender and poignant. Although she was deeply relieved and thankful that her new baby was, in her words, 'here to stay', there was something about the noisy, assertive way this infant laid claim to life that felt overwhelming at times, and could leave this mother feeling irrationally angry.

When another child is born parents can find themselves looking for characteristics in their new child that are similar to and remind them of the child who has died, and these can be both welcome and unwelcome. After his son Josh died at eighteen months Ben found himself searching his newborn son for similarities, and when he did see something, perhaps a particular smile, or the way he screamed at bath time, he could allow himself to believe for a moment that the terrible events had never happened. He needed a moment of solace, if only transitory. It was inevitably followed by the more complex feelings of pain that the past stood unchanged, and then pleasure in the hope that this new child brought. Ben also spoke about wanting others to look at his new son and say how like Josh he was, not especially because he wanted the likeness, but more that he needed to hear people say Josh's name.

One of the more complex losses I encountered as a counsellor was when a mother gave birth to twins, one of whom lived whilst the other died. Parents have to find a way of managing the opposing emotions of sadness and joy. There are often more complicating factors too. It may be that the twin who dies shortly after birth will have, understandably, consumed a considerable amount of the parents' attention before the death, whilst the surviving twin is given less time. This may mean that the mother forms a stronger bond with the child who dies, and then feels guilty and struggles to create a connection with her living child. At times the surviving twin may also be unwell, and together with the grief for the lost twin parents have to manage a high level of anxiety about their surviving child. The complexity of the situation can make it difficult for friends and family to know how to be with the parents. Should they send a card expressing congratulations and another expressing sympathy? How can they best hold and support the parents in such a contradictory situation?

Added sorrow for the parents is the sense that the surviving twin is bereft, and imagining the pain in one so new to the world is hard to bear. The surviving twin may physically carry reminders of the lost twin, particularly if they were identical. The parents, when gazing at their baby, will see the lost child mirrored. For some and at some times this can be a comfort; but for others it is distressing. What it means, though, is that the surviving twin will always be a part of the parents' ongoing connection with their lost child. And if the twin died on the day they were both born birthdays and anniversaries are forever linked.

Chapter 8

HOW BROTHERS AND SISTERS HELP PARENTS STRENGTHEN THE BOND

And somewhere between the years-and-a-half,
When the sky would skip and the sun would laugh,
When the yard was the sea and the wall was the land,
When the whole wide world could fit in a hand.
We sang, we played, we sought, we found.
We teased, we joked, we gathered around,
We wrote, we read, we built, we drew,
Before the years-and-a-half all flew Away.

Karl Jenkins, *Cantata Memoria for the Children* (2016),
written to commemorate the fiftieth anniversary
of the Aberfan disaster, the collapse of a colliery
spoil tip that killed 116 children and 28 adults

One morning I was asked to meet a young couple who were in the paediatric Accident and Emergency department of the hospital having earlier that morning lost their two-year-old daughter from a sudden and catastrophic viral infection. The parents wanted to know what support would be available to them and also how to explain what had happened to their daughter's identical twin sister, who was with them in the hospital. Having spent some time with them I offered to accompany them to the hospital bereavement centre where they could book an appointment to register their little girl's death with the registrar who did a weekly session at the hospital. We used a hospital lift to take us to the second floor. One wall was mirrored. The mother held the surviving twin daughter in her arms, and as this little girl looked up she saw her reflection in the mirror. Believing it to be her sister, her face lit up and she stretched out her arms, giving a cry of joy. It was one of the most poignant moments I experienced in my time at the hospital.

Siblings will carry 50 per cent of the same genetic material as the child who has died, and so in their appearance and personality bring strong associations and sad reminders. But siblings also give wonderful glimpses of the child who has gone, and more, parents describe a refreshing openness and frankness in the ways they speak about their brother or sister who has died. Younger children are less constrained by the carefulness and awkwardness we learn as we grow older. All of this strengthens and nurtures the bonds between parents and their lost child.

But along with this openness, siblings are grieving too, and one of the first concerns many bereaved parents express is how to explain to brothers and sisters what has happened, and how best to support them. The days when death was not spoken about to children and when they were excluded from mourning rituals and funerals have thankfully passed. It was always good to welcome brothers and sisters to the Time to Remember services held at the hospital. Over the period of their sibling's illness and death, other children in the family often feel excluded or marginalised: understandably their parents' orientation at these times is almost exclusively around the needs of the dying child. So to be included in the planning of the funeral and in decisions about where and how their brother or sister will be remembered, and to receive a candle of their own at the Time to Remember service, is very important.

Parents may find it difficult enough themselves to put into words what has happened, and explaining it to a sibling in a way that is appropriate to their age and understanding can be daunting. Nonetheless other children in the family need to be told truthfully and calmly; if some information is omitted the risk is children will fill in the gaps themselves, often with a more frightening version. Also, if the circumstances of the death are not properly explained, children can over-generalise: 'If my sister can die, then I might too, or maybe Mummy and Daddy will die.' If there is any suggestion of information being hidden or avoided, children may wonder who they can now trust in the family, at a time when they will be more than ever looking to their parents for reassurance.

Parents sometimes asked me to advise them about what to say to their other children. The best advice I was given, which I passed on to parents, was to first find a way of asking the child what they already knew and wondered. It is surprising how much children pick up through listening to the conversations of those around them, and this is a good base on which to build a truthful and fuller explanation.

Sometimes brothers and sisters are present when their sibling dies, and when death is expected this can make the months ahead easier. But this may not always be possible, and some children may find it simply too distressing to be there.

Parents wanted to know whether it would be appropriate for children to be taken to see their sibling after the child had died. We rarely felt we could give a definitive answer: so much depended on what the parents felt most comfortable with, and how they perceived the sensibilities of their children. The decision for siblings to see their brother or sister was clearer if the child who had died had been unwell for some time and the death was expected; siblings would be more prepared for the death and may have been involved in conversations about it beforehand. Perhaps it also seemed clearer when the death was of a baby who was newly born and who had not yet been seen by the other children in the family. Meeting this new family member, if only to say goodbye, could be really important for the siblings' understanding that a baby had actually been born. A decision for siblings not to see their brother or sister who had died was clearer if the child's body was disfigured by an accident or disease.

When Jacob's little sister Bethan died in hospital at the age of two months, Jacob, who was four, was familiar with the hospital life, staff and routines. He had more or less lived there with his mother throughout his baby sister's short life. On the morning she died Jacob went to the hospital school, drew pictures for Bethan and some for his mother, and then sat with his mother while she cuddled Bethan and read to him, before saying goodbye to his little sister. This period of his life had come to an end, but the ending was in many ways no different from the other days. Bethan's presence in his life and her parting from it had been as gentle and natural as it could be.

However, despite the openness and greater inclusion of brothers and sisters, the impact of a sibling's death on children in the family is considerable. Over the period when parents have no choice but to focus almost exclusively on their dying child's needs and the arrangements that have to be made, other children in the family may be cared for by the extended family or friends, and however loving and familiar that care is, the routine and security of everyday family life is disrupted. Riches and Dawson write about the needs of siblings, following an extensive study of bereaved families. Their research indicated that, for a number of children, a sibling's death 'irrevocably changed their family and made their own place within it less secure' (Riches and Dawson 2000, p.3). The 'hole in the domestic landscape where the child used to be', together with the preoccupation of the parents with the dead child, can leave surviving children feeling bewildered and bereft (p.6). But, as it is with parents, not all bereaved siblings are affected in the same way. Much will depend on their age and position in the family when the loss occurs, and how they are listened to and supported. Riches and Dawson remind the reader that for some the loss can 'contribute to immense emotional growth and appreciation of the value of life' (p.76).

There are useful books and resources (available from organisations such as The Compassionate Friends, Winston's Wish and Child Bereavement UK) written specifically for bereaved siblings, and there are opportunities, through organisations such as Winston's Wish, for children to attend special events where they can think through what has happened with other bereaved children and adults. See the Resources section at the end of the book for details of these and other organisations.

What we know is helpful for siblings is the opportunity to say goodbye, either in reality or symbolically if the former is not realistic, for their ongoing routines to be disrupted as little as possible, and for them to be given as much information as is appropriate for their age. They should be encouraged to express their feelings, through talking, writing, drawing and playing, and if their family enjoys good social support, a chance to have a range of others to talk to. This can provide a sometimes needed escape from the intensity of the home environment and help with feelings of isolation and stigma.

When her brother Joe died, Denise's six-year-old daughter initiated the making of a memory box. Not wanting photographs and any of Joe's personal effects visible in the home, with the help of her mother she chose a large wooden box and amongst other things she placed in it some of his toys, his birth certificate, his shoes and his toothbrush. She then decorated the box and took it into school to show her class. It was as if instinctively she knew what would be helpful for her, and her mother's attunement to her daughter's needs meant that they were met (Turner 2014a).

As it becomes increasingly uncommon for a child to die, so it is rare for a sibling to have a friend or someone in their school who has experienced the same. So it is especially important that teachers are able to help children explain what has happened to their peers. Through being encouraged to talk about their loss to others, children often find they can start to understand it better for themselves. And their peers benefit from hearing something that can be frightening and confusing spoken about openly.

Maddie's family always looked for her star at night. When the family travelled, at bedtime her three younger siblings would look upwards to find Maddie's star wherever they were, so that they could say goodnight. The children were always able to identify it with absolute certainty.

In families where the child who has died is spoken about and remembered sadly but easily, children in the family may offer new insights and ways of remembering. Leanne was born after her sister Isabel had died, but nonetheless her mother heard her boasting to her older sister that actually she had been Isabel's best friend!

Andrew was born a year after his sister Hannah died. Hannah's mother writes, 'Hannah is still such a big part of our lives, even though she's not here. We talk about her all the time, even Andrew speaks about her – it's really lovely.'

How siblings are supported and involved will be influenced by factors such as their age and whether they are older or younger than their brother or sister who has died, whether the child died suddenly and unexpectedly, or whether they had been living in a family with a sibling who had a life-limiting illness or disability. For children who have been living with a sibling who has been unwell, family life will have been centered on the needs of that child, with all the mixed feelings that can bring. I was often impressed by parents' descriptions of the strong expressions of loyalty and protectiveness siblings showed, and how the inevitable limitations to normal family life and compromises that were required were accepted with good grace.

Sometimes the need to explain to and support siblings gives parents a chance to work through some of their own feelings. When her baby died of a heart condition at the age of three months, Alison was concerned for her older child, Charlie, who was just over two. He was, she felt, too young to be able to properly articulate how he felt and bewildered by the sudden disappearance of his new sister. In the weeks after she died Alison devoted herself to the creation of a special book for Charlie all about his sister. With photographs and simple text the book told the story of her brief life from the perspective of her older brother. Once completed, Alison shared the book with Charlie, who at first showed only a little interest, but as the months passed would sometimes choose it to be read to him. When he reached an age when he was reading more complex texts he would still select this special book from time to time. Sometimes reading it facilitated conversations about his sister, other times it didn't. Occasionally Charlie would choose to stop the reading before the part where his sister died.

The making of the book was important to Alison in the early weeks of her loss; she valued thinking about the text and selecting the photographs for it. Because it was so simply written it spoke directly, and that helped her begin to take in what had occurred. As she shared it with her son, she welcomed the chance to think and talk about her daughter. Alison describes the book as 'a family testament for our remaining children, to be taken up at any stage of their lives'.

The counselling service at the hospital didn't provide counselling for siblings. My colleague and I were not trained to work with children. We were able to refer some siblings to the paediatric psychology service or signpost parents to local services. But brothers and sisters were very present in our work with parents.

Grace, at thirteen, was an only child. She and her parents had a close and happy relationship, but Grace longed for a sister. She had almost given up hope when her mother became pregnant. The pregnancy was difficult and baby Verity was born very prematurely. She was cared for in the neonatal intensive care unit but there was little hope that she would live. Grace and her father visited Verity every day and Grace was able to help her mother with the small tasks of caring for Verity that were possible. After Verity died Grace held her and was allowed to choose what the family would dress her in. She was greatly affected by all this, and being included was important. Being exposed to her little sister's vulnerability touched something in Grace which she then transformed and expressed in caring for her mother when she returned from the hospital. In the early days this gave her a sense of purpose and her mother valued it deeply. Mother, father and Grace became even closer, bonded by grief and sharing something so sad and so significant. This enabled Grace to continue to manage well at school, and as the months passed and Grace could see her mother becoming stronger and return to work, Grace was able to become the child again in the family. This was a family who already had in place a supportive and secure system, who when challenged by distress were able to develop new ways of caring for each other without the system becoming stressed. Their continuing bond with Verity was both individually held and mutually shared.

When a family system is less secure and has been through recent changes, bereaved siblings may have more of a struggle. Rebekah was brought up by her mother, her father having left shortly after she was born. When Rebekah was ten her mother had a new partner and not long into the relationship became pregnant. Rebekah seemed to settle well into this new family arrangement and was very excited about having a new baby brother, Olly. Tragically, Olly died from meningitis at the age of fourteen months, very suddenly, whilst Rebekah was staying over at a friend's house. At the time her mother and her partner had been glad that Rebekah had been spared the fright and horror of Olly's sudden collapse and the paramedics coming to the home, but it was bewildering for Rebekah to unexpectedly have her sleepover extended by another day and night and then to return home to learn that Olly had died. Her mother's partner became depressed and preoccupied by his first child's death. He found it difficult to have Rebekah around him. Rebekah's mother had to manage supporting her daughter and her partner and caring for herself; a task that was made even more difficult by the unexpected death of her mother. Rebekah withdrew from family life, spending more time with friends. She became involved in a group who were missing school. Her mother felt helpless and bereft; it was as if she had lost two children. It was very difficult for any of the family to develop a continuing bond with Olly whilst current and immediate family concerns were so preoccupying. It was only after a period of family therapy and individual support for Rebekah that the family were able to become cohesive and strong enough to begin grieving.

Martha lived with her father Tim and her younger brother Sam. Their mother had died shortly after Sam's birth and Tim had brought up Martha and Sam as a single father. At the age of eight Sam was diagnosed with a life-limiting illness which brought about a gradual deterioration in his mental and physical abilities. His father looked after him at home, with the support of the local hospice, until Sam died at the age of twelve. During this period, although Sam's needs and behaviour dominated family life, Martha, who was thirteen when her brother was diagnosed, found a way of both being there for her father and Sam at home and navigating adolescence, school, exams and a transfer to college with great resilience and determination. This family had evidently developed a strong supportive system following the death of the children's mother which, despite the challenge of Sam's illness and then death, continued to be effective.

Martha grew very close to Sam in the months before he died, and together with their father they shared a happy and memorable time away together at the seaside. They worked together to store up shared memories from which Martha and Tim were later able to draw strength. For this family humour always played a key role, and although I didn't get to see Tim very often, because it was difficult for him to leave Sam to come to the hospital, I always found my telephone conversations with him to be a mix of sad and amusing anecdotes about the challenges of life with Sam.

After Sam died both Martha and her father drew comfort from their strong continuing bond with him. This was founded on the good communication they had always enjoyed as a family, a positivity which had held them through very challenging times and the laughter and love of life which the three of them had often shared. Just as Tim would always be the father of a son, so too Martha would never stop being a sister.

Chapter 9

WHAT MIGHT GET IN THE WAY OF PARENTS BEING ABLE TO ESTABLISH A CONTINUING BOND?

Most of what I have written so far has been about how bereaved parents find ways of creating and building a bond with their child after death. What I hope to have shown are the many varied and creative ways parents do this, although I imagine the process of and motivation for doing so is largely subconscious. Few parents would say, 'I am doing this, writing this, joining this, speaking about this…because I want to strengthen the continuing bond with my lost child.'

The stories I have shared have been of parents who have found ways of doing this that, although terribly painful, have been as natural as breathing. Their instincts have been to transform the relationship from one that has been based on a physical presence to one that is psychological, emotional and often spiritual. But it would be wrong to ignore that for some parents, and maybe for most, there are times when things get in the way of the ongoing connection feeling present, secure and meaningful. What can threaten and weaken the bond? From what I have learned from parents I would suggest it is guilt, anger and conflict. I also have a sense that establishing a secure, meaningful continuing bond may be more difficult for parents who have pre-existing mental health issues or problems to do with attachment.

When parents feel guilty

Most of the bereaved parents I worked with spoke about feelings of guilt arising from specific decisions they made, events that had occurred, or a sense of having failed their children by not being able to protect them. Mothers who had a stillbirth or gave birth to a premature baby who didn't survive might express a belief that their body had failed. Parents told me they believed they must have done something wrong to be punished by God in this way. Some might say this in one breath and in the next say that their child had been specially chosen by God to be with Him, believing their child's death to be both punishment and blessing.

Over time most parents acknowledged that these thoughts and feelings had little or no base in reason; decisions had been guided by their child's best interests and they had always done their utmost to protect and nurture their child. But for some parents, being able to believe this was more difficult.

Daniel came for counselling a few months after his son Christopher died. Christopher was born with a severe heart abnormality and was a fragile baby. Surgery was planned for when he was three months old and a little bigger and stronger, but he died from a chest infection before it could take place. Daniel and his wife Eleanor were distraught. It seemed that the ray of hope they had been clinging on to since Christopher's birth had been there only to deceive, and they felt cheated. However, over time Eleanor accepted that Christopher would not have been strong enough to cope with surgery any sooner and that the decisions they and the consultant cardiac surgeon had made together had been wise and appropriate.

Daniel found it harder to accept. Although he knew that he and Eleanor had cared for their son in every possible way, nonetheless he felt responsible for his son's death and was exhausted by feelings of guilt. In counselling Daniel explored with me over and over the decisions that had been made, and whether anything should have been done differently. But although he would find himself concurring that everyone had acted in the best possible way, his guilt remained undiminished and was so consuming that he could hardly bear to talk about his son other than in this context. This impacted on his relationship with Eleanor who, at a time when she was needing to feel close to Daniel more than anything, found him withdrawn and uncommunicative.

As the weeks progressed what began to emerge were Daniel's profound feelings of responsibility for his family. His mother had suffered from severe depression, and when he was growing up his father was the person who gave strength and security to the family. As a new father Daniel assumed the role of being the one in the family who took all responsibility to protect them, even though he had a partner with considerable emotional strength and resilience. Becoming a father had connected Daniel with his own experience of fatherhood, and when Christopher died he believed he had failed. Unpicking these beliefs helped Daniel understand better why he had thought this way, and this enabled him to begin to feel less guilty. He started to be able to talk more easily about Christopher and remember him with sadness that did not leave him knotted inside.

Anthony's son Luke was diagnosed with kidney disease at the age of six and had to have regular dialysis. A transplant was unsuccessful and Luke became weak and vulnerable to infections, but was able to be at home when he was not having dialysis. He needed to be admitted for a simple routine operation and was very anxious. Anthony did his best to reassure him, promising him that it was much less complicated surgery than he had had before and that all would be well. Tragically Luke's heart failed immediately after the surgery and he didn't wake up from the anaesthetic. Although Anthony had known that his son's life was limited, he had never imagined it would end in this way, with him not present and having given Luke what he now believed to be false promises. He also felt the responsibility of having given his consent for surgery. Surgery, however, had been essential and Anthony knew that he had had no choice. But it took some time for him to accept that he had done what was best for his child, and time too for Anthony to disentangle guilt from his grief.

However, sometimes parents' choices turn out with hindsight not to have been the best choices, even though they were made with the very best intentions. Gloria chose to have a home birth for her third child. Her first two had been born in hospital and both deliveries had been straightforward. She was encouraged to have a home birth by her GP and the community midwives, but her friends and neighbours did not think it was a good idea. Gloria lived in a close-knit community where hospital births were favoured over home deliveries. But Gloria felt confident to follow the advice of the professionals, in spite of persistent questioning from her friends and neighbours.

Things began to go wrong when Gloria was two weeks overdue. Missing notes and miscommunications coincided with a weekend when there were staff shortages. As a consequence, by the time Gloria's labour began spontaneously her baby's heart rate had probably been slowing down for some time. The home birth went wrong and the baby boy, Kai, was born floppy and unresponsive. He was taken to a neonatal intensive care unit, but died three days later. Gloria was distraught and overwhelmed by guilt. She believed she had made a serious error in choosing a home birth and that she should have been more assertive when her baby was overdue. She avoided her friends and neighbours who she believed would blame her, was unable to return to work and became severely depressed. Throughout the period of the inquest and subsequent legal action she remained deeply troubled and distressed, and had a brief admission to a psychiatric hospital. Gloria could not stop replaying over and over the pregnancy and the birth, blaming herself for each decision that she and others had made. It was all she could think about.

An extended period of counselling, support from the bereaved parents' group and the loving concern of a close friend helped Gloria to start to accept she had acted in what she had held to be the best interests of her baby. The mistakes were made by others, and the responsibility for what had gone so badly wrong lay with them. This was endorsed eventually by the outcome of the legal process. Gloria continued to feel very deeply the loss of Kai, but she began to also be able to think about him as the baby she had loved and lost, and to find a quieter way of holding him in her heart.

In recent years science has made great advances in the field of genetics. Our growing knowledge and the development of increasingly sophisticated genetic testing have brought benefits to parents who carry a genetically linked condition. Parents who have a family history of a genetic disorder and those in certain ethnic groups who have an increased risk of specific genetic conditions can sometimes be tested prior to conception and given information about their risk of having a child with that condition. Diagnostic genetic testing can be used to confirm a diagnosis in a symptomatic parent or child, and parents of children who have an inherited condition can be given information about the risk to future children, and be informed about whether one parent or both carry the altered gene. Prenatal diagnosis may be an option that they may wish to consider in any future pregnancy.

In some situations pre-implantation genetic diagnosis (in vitro fertilisation followed by a biopsy of the embryo and genetic testing) can be used to select an unaffected embryo which can be re-implanted, significantly reducing the risk of a resulting pregnancy having a specific genetic or chromosomal disorder.

Sometimes a genetic condition arises as the result of a new mutation in the child, and neither parent is a carrier. This significantly reduces the risk in a future pregnancy. In any family where there has been a genetic diagnosis, or the possibility is raised, referral to a genetics centre should be encouraged.

A potential drawback of these developments is that when a child dies because of a genetically linked or chromosomal condition, often parents will now know who carried the genetic material that caused this (it may also be neither of them or both). We all carry altered genes, and for most of us the consequences are not noticeable or significant. But if we are carriers of a gene that has had such a severe consequence for our child, then it is difficult not to feel responsible. Sometimes the parent who is the carrier of the altered gene will think that their partner blames them, and perhaps hardest of all, sometimes the partner does blame them.

Blame in a situation where there are no grounds for it is very hard to bear, especially when it tunes in to an existing sense of guilt and responsibility. The truth is that none of us is responsible for our genes, and rationally we know this. But when emotions are very high and grief very deep, rational thoughts can be difficult to find.

What is even harder (and this is perhaps one of the hardest things to think and write about) is when a parent does have some degree of responsibility for their child's death. For parents describing the events leading to their child's death there are always the 'what if?' questions. These can be to do with timing: 'Why didn't I take my child straight to

Accident and Emergency rather than to the GP first?' 'Why did I wait until the morning to call the GP?' And they are sometimes to do with being assertive enough: 'Why didn't I insist that my child was too unwell to be sent home?' 'Why didn't I insist that we saw a consultant in Accident and Emergency rather than a junior doctor?' They may also be to do with the parents' own knowledge and assessment of a situation: 'Why didn't I notice that she was struggling to breathe?' 'Why didn't I take his complaint about a chest pain after playing football more seriously?'

In most of these situations the delays, the lack of assertiveness and the slowness to pick up that there was a serious problem would not have affected the outcome. But occasionally it might. And that can be devastating for a parent to accept, and devastating too when a partner is not present when those decisions were taken.

Most difficult of all to think about are the children who die because of a parent's carelessness, neglect or deliberate action. Yet all parents know that when we are under stress there are times when momentarily we don't give our children our full attention. For most of us there are no consequences, but for just a few tragically there are: a child drowns in the bath, a child runs out across the road, a child swallows a cell battery. In my experience, those of us who are parents have no problem in extending a hand and saying, 'That could have happened to my child; you are no more blameworthy than any parent.' But the parents for whom this happens usually find it impossible to find even the smallest grain of forgiveness for themselves, certainly not until some considerable time has passed.

In my experience these parents find it very difficult to come to counselling; perhaps it is that they don't want to return to the hospital and are seeking other help elsewhere. I hope so. Nor do they come to the group, even though

I know that the parents there would be the first to offer understanding and acceptance.

When parents feel angry

Death leaves those left behind angry. Even when it comes at the end of a long life, or as a relief after pain and suffering, those who have loved and lost feel anger within their grief. We have been abandoned, left to pick up and reorganise the pieces of our lives without a person who should be there. We are angry with a world where loss is inevitable, unavoidable and beyond our control.

So it is understandable that parents who lose a child are very angry: incandescent and railing at the world where the rules have been broken. Many parents will say, 'I never imagined I would bury my own child. It is just wrong.'

Because it is difficult to be angry with something as abstract and intangible as the world, parents may express anger with God. Or they will be angry with hospital staff, the coroner, their friends and family, with each other or themselves. Being angry is normal and important; it is part of the whole range of overwhelming emotions bereaved parents experience.

But parents' anger becomes concerning and can be disabling when it eclipses the story of their child's life; when it is all a parent can think or speak about. Then it can severely disrupt and distort growing an ongoing bond with their child.

When a child dies parents are always left with unanswered questions. Conversations with doctors around the time of the child's death happen, but rarely are parents able to take in much of their content, because the circumstances are just too distressing. At the hospital it was important that parents were invited to meet within a few weeks after their child's death the consultants who had been responsible for their child's care. As counsellors we arranged and hosted these meetings. They gave parents the chance to go over the decisions that had been made regarding their child's treatment and care and to ask questions. Most parents who accepted this invitation came with questions they hadn't yet asked and questions that had been addressed before but needed going through again.

Sometimes parents came feeling angry and upset about a decision that had been taken, but with explanation were able to see that the best possible decision had been made. However, very occasionally the explanations were very difficult to give and for parents to hear, because just sometimes decisions had been made that in retrospect might not have been the best.

My experience was that most parents were grateful for the honesty of the doctors and knew that decisions were always made with the utmost concern for the best outcome for the child. So when these painful conversations were open and honest, and parents were willing to see that their child had been the paramount concern, they were able to leave with a greater understanding and feeling less angry. Henry Marsh, a neurosurgeon, writes candidly about the times he has made surgical errors which have had devastating consequences for his patients and their families: '…if you do not hide or deny any mistakes when things go wrong, and if your patients and their families know that you are distressed by whatever happened, you might, if you are lucky, receive the precious gift of forgiveness' (Marsh 2014, p.180).

But some parents, who perhaps felt too upset to come to the meeting, or who were not helped by the conversation, remained angry. And when parents felt that errors had been made that were not justifiable and legal procedures begun, anger remained a powerful and dominant emotion for months and sometimes years to come.

Pam and Adrian's three-year-old daughter Della died as a consequence of a misdiagnosis and consequent delay in proper treatment at their local hospital. The couple were referred to our service for counselling because Della had been known to our hospital and because they refused to return to the hospital where she had died. Two months after Della's death I met with both parents. For the whole of the first meeting neither parent was able to speak about anything other than their rage at the hospital where Della had died. This feeling of great injustice dominated their thoughts.

When a child dies in these circumstances it is likely that friends and family will have heard the story and experienced the depth of the parents' anger. Wanting to be helpful and supportive, they will have shared the parents' outrage. In counselling the couple are given a different experience; their story is heard with concern and sensitivity, but the counsellor does not join in an outpouring of anger (that is not to say that when we hear descriptions of unacceptable levels of care, we do not feel angry).

Following this first meeting Adrian did not return, saying that counselling had not been at all helpful. His partner Pam was less sure, and after a hesitant start, when she did not always attend an arranged meeting, she eventually made a commitment to coming regularly. And although nothing lessened the fact that a terrible thing had happened to her child, which should never have happened, she found it helpful to talk about Della's life and her loss in a more reflective way. Adrian remained paralysed by his anger. An inquest and subsequent legal action meant that the outside world's focus seemed to be entirely on the cause of Della's death.

Adrian became depressed and started to drink. He wouldn't seek help from his GP, because he now believed that no one in the medical profession could be trusted, and eventually he lost his job. Sadly Pam and Adrian's older child, Tim, who had just started at secondary school and had been doing well, was affected by his father's moods and was also grieving his sister. He began to miss school and isolate himself from his friends. My sessions with Pam became increasingly focused around her concerns for Adrian and Tim, and Della became pushed to the edges. The tragedy was that the anger this family felt, and its impact on their lives, meant that any ongoing bond with Della was entirely coloured by a sense of injustice and pain.

When there is conflict between parents

Pam and Antonio's first child Eli died at the age of eighteen months after a long illness. Most of his short life was spent on a hospital ward and his mother was with him all the time. But Antonio had to work, and as the family lived some distance from the hospital, he could only be with his wife and child at weekends. Pam's relationship with her little boy consequently became very intense, and Antonio often felt excluded when he was with them. Because most of the conversations with doctors occurred during the week, Antonio was rarely part of them, and he was less in touch with the decisions that were being made about Eli's care. It was Pam who gradually understood that it was unlikely that Eli would be well enough to live at home, and that his life was limited. Although she spoke about this with Antonio, he could not accept it.

When Eli died Pam grieved deeply but she had known for a long time that this was going to happen. Antonio was incredulous, disbelieving and angry. He thought that Pam was not sufficiently upset and accused her of not loving Eli as much as he did. Pam blamed Antonio for not being there for Eli when he was alive, and for her when she needed his support. The couple's relationship became increasingly acrimonious, and because each time they spoke about Eli to each other the wounds were reopened, they avoided it.

Pam became pregnant and hoped that a new child would make the relationship closer again. But when a daughter was born Antonio was unable to feel anything for her. He had held on to the hope that this baby would be like Eli and was unable to cope with her not being like him. Shortly after the birth the couple separated.

My colleague and I didn't often see parents who separated after the death of their child. It may be that they didn't use our counselling services, or it may be that although parents will often talk about difficulties in their relationship, especially those arising from their different ways of grieving, relationship breakdown after the loss of a child happened to only a few. Riches and Dawson write about the breakdown of couple relationships following the death of a child, and from their own studies and the research of others conclude that whilst a child's death might put a couple's relationship under considerable stress, equally it might bring about an increased closeness. Overall there seemed to be no evidence to suggest that bereaved couples have a greater incidence of relationship breakdown than couples who have not lost a child (Riches and Dawson 2000).

When a child dies parents go through possibly the most difficult experience they will have ever had to manage together, a time when they are making decisions about things that are rarely spoken about. Do you want to visit our child in the mortuary once more? Shall we have our child buried or cremated? What shall we tell others, and who will do the telling? How shall we plan a funeral? After an intense period of joint decision making, and shared and public grief, parents may withdraw into a time of more personal grieving.

We all grieve differently, and it is the same for couples. We grieve collectively with friends, family and community and we grieve individually. Grief has a personal rhythm, focus and pace. At times how one parent grieves may not sit easily with the other. One may need to talk, the other may need solitude. One's grief may seem too intense, the other's not intense enough. A parent's grief may appear excluding of the other or unboundaried. Differences at a time when parents need to feel close to each other can be distressing and confusing. Riches and Dawson call this the 'paradox of child death' (Riches and Dawson 2000, p.4). It is usually the family we turn to when facing extreme difficulty, and yet when a child dies those who would normally be there for us are suffering too. We can feel isolated from our most intimate relationships when we need them the most. Developing an ongoing bond with the lost child that is shared and mutual can be difficult.

There were occasions when my colleague or I would see a couple following the death of their child and decide with them that it might be better for them to be seen individually, at least for a time. We were aware that even with close couples there were times when each would gain from some personal space to talk without having to be sensitive to a partner's feelings. This is both important to the person who is doing the talking, but also to the partner, who may be relieved to know that their partner is being looked after.

When there is conflict with a hospital

For some parents the death of their child leads to a long, complex and often acrimonious legal dispute with the hospital, when decisions that were made about the child's treatment and care are believed to have been wrong and possibly contributory to the death. When there are waits for inquests, when inquests are adjourned pending more information and when legal procedures are started, parents can find themselves in a process that may take several years to resolve. They can then feel as if their grief is held in limbo. Victims of other traumatic events awaiting legal decisions regarding compensation are reported to have similar experiences of being emotionally stuck, unable to process the trauma and its accompanying psychological impact. Feelings of anger, helplessness and injustice can take hold. This can be functional in that the impact of the trauma remains very present and therefore easier to demonstrate, and for some it can be energising. But it comes at a cost.

On occasions my colleague and I were asked to see parents whose child had been known to our hospital but who were in a legal process with another hospital. Sometimes a child who was well known to our hospital died elsewhere.

Aaron and Cally's two-year-old son Jake died in hospital when they were on holiday in another part of the country. Jake had a heart condition and was under the care of our hospital. Aaron and Cally strongly believed that Jake died because of a failure to properly respond to the complex needs of their child and decided to take legal action. Aaron was a lawyer and decided to prepare as much as he could of the complaint himself, and over the subsequent two years immersed himself in this process. In addition to the mental space this claimed for both parents, the couple's physical space gradually became filled with papers, until it seemed that their whole house, except for Jake's room which remained untouched, was filled with documentation and files. Aaron saw me for counselling from time to time over this period, and although he expressed concern about this situation, he felt unable to do anything to change it. Outside, the grass in the garden grew until it reached the windows.

Aaron and Cally were paralysed by this process. It was as if in trying to restore a sense of agency, after feeling so helpless when Jake died, they were instead recreating their experience of feeling overwhelmed and stuck. But even though at times Aaron despaired of ever seeing the process through, he eventually succeeded in reaching a settlement with the hospital where Jake had died, with the hospital admitting responsibility. The couple gradually began to create space in both their internal and external worlds. The lawn was mown and they began to grieve for Jake.

When there are pre-existing difficulties

Death occurs in lives that have a history. Some parents who are bereaved are already living lives that are painful and challenging. Some will have come to parenting with a background of difficult and unhappy childhood experiences of their own. For many this will have affected the relationship they had with the child they have lost. 'A parent's ability to survive emotionally will be impacted by what has gone before in their lives, by their own childhood experiences of parenting itself and by what they have invested in their relationship with their child' (Chalmers 2007, p.4).

How we form attachments with our children is influenced by our early experience. People who have had strong and secure early attachments are likely to find it easier to form similar bonds with their own children. And when there is a secure, close attachment in life, then this kind of bond is easier to recreate in death. But not everyone comes to parenthood having had a good experience of being parented themselves, and those who have not may find it challenging to build confident and happy relationships with their children. Some are troubled by anxiety or insecurity, others by simply not having known kind, selfless parental love. For some parents very real problems of living, coming from circumstances such as financial hardship, mental or physical ill health, isolation or domestic violence, can make it difficult to build and enjoy happy and secure relationships with their children.

It is unsurprising that for parents who are already living with these challenges, continuing a meaningful bond with their child after death can be more difficult. Their life circumstances will not have changed, the loss will have made them far sadder, and they are less likely to have the resilience and loving support to help them grieve.

When it is difficult to form helpful, trusting attachments, it is not easy to seek out counselling, so inevitably my colleague and I rarely saw parents who were struggling to this degree, except maybe for a one-off meeting. These parents tended not to want to come back. Perhaps some found help in the less personal Time to Remember services; I hope so.

I remember seeing a bereaved mother over an extended period who became deeply depressed. She had lost her only child, and as she was in her mid-forties the possibility of becoming pregnant again was less likely. She did become pregnant again, but suffered an early miscarriage, was unable to continue to work, and her relationship broke down. I was very concerned when she began to express suicidal thoughts and with her agreement worked with her GP to arrange an admission to a psychiatric ward, where she was treated for clinical depression. The loss of her child had woken memories of past losses and triggered further losses, and in the very dark place she found herself she could find no meaning or comfort in a notion of a continuing bond, at least for that period in her life.

Perhaps it is just as difficult for those whose identity as parents is so total that it is the only way they define themselves as an adult. When that is lost they may replace their identity as a mother or father with that of being a bereaved parent. I was concerned for parents who seemed immersed in this identity to the exclusion of almost all else. In a way, paradoxically it seemed to work against an ongoing bond with their child because the relationship became so static. But I am mindful that in this, as in all the examples I have given of the challenges to creating an ongoing bond, there will be an element of my own judgement. And this is something about which we all – friends, family and professionals – need to be sensitive.

Chapter 10

CAN THE CONTINUING BOND BE A SOURCE OF NEW ENERGY AND STRENGTH?

I have been doing things I would never have done: I talk to complete strangers, I allow my curiosity greater rein; I have taken myself to places I would never have gone to, both physical and cerebral; I have embraced the idea, a doctrine almost, of 'why not?'

Oliver Wingate, *A Letter to Henry* (2010), written to his son after his death at the age of 24 in a road traffic accident (privately published)

Mattie's father Danny is a musician and composer. When Mattie died at four of a heart condition he had been born with, Danny and his partner mourned deeply. In the early weeks Danny sought refuge in music, both playing and writing, and out of the place where his pain resided Danny found a powerful creative energy. He wrote what he believed to be his best composition in memory of his son. He said that it was as if his pain had stripped him bare and from this vulnerability came a purity and clarity he had not before known.

Jackie worked in investment banking. When she was pregnant she was told that her baby had Down syndrome and an associated severe heart abnormality. Jackie decided not to take maternity leave, but to give up work and devote her time to caring for her daughter. She researched widely how best to support and encourage the learning and development of a child with Down syndrome and felt excited about and committed to the challenges and joys that lay ahead. Sadly, her little girl, Kate, died at nine months. Jackie knew even before Kate's death that she had changed, and could not return to her previous career. She retrained as a teacher for children with special needs. This new direction gave Jackie a sense that her own life now had more meaning, and in her day-to-day work she felt close to Kate.

Stuart told me that after his son Toby died he no longer feared his own death: 'How can I be afraid to go where my son has already gone ahead of me? If he can do it, then I can too.'

Madeleine and Tim's daughter Avril died from meningitis at the age of three. She had been profoundly deaf since birth and her parents learned subsequently that this had put her at a higher risk of contracting meningitis. They were angry that this information had not been given to them when she was born as they believed that with that knowledge they might have been more alert to possible symptoms. For some, anger can be paralysing, but for Madeleine and Tim anger was galvanising and they became involved in supporting Meningitis Now, the UK's largest meningitis charity. Further, before Avril died Madeleine and Tim had trained in signing in order to be able to communicate with their daughter. After Avril died Madeleine used her skills as an interpreter for the deaf at the local benefits advisory service; she felt that this would honour Avril's life. Working with people who were deaf also gave her connectedness with Avril that she hadn't anticipated.

Parents I worked with spoke of being significantly changed by their child's death. Bereaved parents will pour great reserves of creative energy into starting or supporting a charity or foundation which is usually connected to the condition that caused their child's death. As well as being beneficial to the cause and to other children and families, this gives a much-needed focus at a time when much has changed. The energy parents have poured into caring for their child can now be directed into something that connects them. Their life has a new reference point and, as one parent pointed out, it is easier to talk enthusiastically to people about fundraising than it is about a child who has died. And very importantly, it means that their children still matter, not just to those who knew them but to a greater community.

The parents I met have run marathons, cycled across deserts and mountains, organised swimming galas, sewn coverlets for the neonatal ward, arranged celebrity dinners, abseiled, set up support groups, arranged fun days on the wards, sold plants outside their garden gate...too many activities to name them all. We read in the national press inspiring stories of parents who, following the loss of a child, have dedicated energy and time to raising awareness and money and influencing government policies.

Marina Fogle, a mother of two, designed an antenatal class with her sister that set out to be both positive and honest about giving birth. She felt that pregnant women were too often exposed to catastrophic birth stories that were both inaccurate and frightening. However, when her third child Willem was stillborn she recognised the importance of being open and honest about the fact that sometimes things go desperately wrong. In a newspaper article she describes how the 'senselessness' of her baby's death has been especially hard to come to terms with, but that the change it wrought in her and what she has done with that has helped to create meaning:

> But if his death can give me a voice to talk about something that people are afraid of talking about, or give a pregnant woman the confidence to seek advice if she has any

questions or concerns about her pregnancy, his death seems a little less pointless and that makes my pain easier to bear. (Fogle 2015, p.3)

Marina is now the patron of MAMA Academy which provides pregnant women with 'Wellbeing Wallets' in which they carry their antenatal notes, providing a means of conveying safer pregnancy information.

Following the loss of her son Adam to childhood cancer at the age of twelve, Susan Hay set up Adam's Hats, a charity which funded research and provided holiday accommodation to families where a child is very sick. Adam's Hats has now become part of the Children's Cancer and Leukaemia Group. Subsequently Susan has become chair of Neuroblastoma UK, a charity that raises money for research and arranges international conferences for researchers and practitioners who are working in the field of childhood cancer. A newspaper magazine article entitled 'Cancer in Children' described the impact of Adam's sudden and devastating illness and death on the whole family, and how, out of this, the loss of one young life, so much has been achieved by the family to influence the treatment and chances of future children. Susan Hay is quoted as saying that she and her fellow campaigners draw succour from the words of the late anthropologist Margaret Mead: 'Never doubt that a small group of thoughtful committed citizens can change the world. Indeed, it's the only thing that ever has' (Roberts 2015).

Many of the bereaved parents I encountered are exactly that.

As I have been writing this chapter, the media's attention has been drawn to the story of two-year-old Faye Burdett who died from Meningitis B (Men B) on 14 February 2016. Her family released a photograph of her just before she died, her body swollen and disfigured by the ravages of sepsis. As a consequence of this courageous and outraged act by the family, 823,000 people signed a petition calling on the government to change NHS provision so that all children receive the Men B vaccine, not just newborn babies. However, the government's decision was and still is that it would not be cost-effective and consequently children and teenagers remain at risk. Despite the decision not to extend the vaccine, Meningitis Now continue to call for the vaccine to be available to all children under the age of five and to families where there has been a case of meningitis.

So the debate continues, and people will remember Faye. The picture was shocking and uncompromising, showing Faye, a vulnerable two-year-old, dying as a consequence of meningitis. Few people will have seen images like these before. Faye's parents took an intimate and tragic family event and made it public in a way that alerted the country to what they believed was an unacceptable ruling on an NHS provision. In those desperate hours just before her death Faye's parents found a way to give her tragedy meaning. At the same time as the petition they set up a link to the online fundraising platform JustGiving, and raised £75,000 in Faye's memory for children's charities. Faye's father spoke to me of the comfort it brought him and his wife to know that Faye's life had 'made a mark'; it made them proud of her.

Meningitis Now, originally called the Meningitis Trust, was created in 1986 following the merger of two smaller support and fundraising groups started by parents and families affected by the disease. Over thirty years this organisation has grown from strength to strength working to raise awareness of the disease, to support families and to fund research into the development and introduction of vaccines. As a consequence of what was originally a small group of parents whose lives had been affected by this disease, large strides have been made both in understanding meningitis, and through the introduction of a number of lifesaving vaccines, including the Hib vaccine against bacterial meningitis in 1992, the Meningococcal C vaccine in 1999, the Pneumococcal meningitis vaccine in 2006 and most recently (2015) the Meningococcal B vaccine for newborn infants and seventeen- and eighteen-year-old teenagers. Meningitis Now gives an important and influential voice to the thousands of people who have experienced the consequences of this feared disease. Its website tells its history and achievements and encourages visitors to become involved in its support and fundraising activities (see the Resources section at the end of this book).

Integral to the high-profile and sophisticated coverage achieved by Meningitis Now are the individual stories shared by parents and families, often of their child's death. They follow a similar path: their child is not themselves, out of sorts, nothing to be too much concerned about. Calpol is given, a GP may be called and reassurance given. The symptoms worsen, the child has a temperature, is sick, and very distressed. This time the GP advises taking the child to Accident and Emergency. Suddenly everything escalates: a rash develops, and within hours the child is dying. It all happens within a day or two. Lives are irreversibly changed.

In all that follows, the chaos, bewilderment, grief and despair, parents want and need to share their child's story with others: not only to raise other parents' awareness (although for some of those who tell their story a raised awareness would not have changed the outcome); not only to change legislation and NHS priorities; not only to pledge to support research initiatives and fundraising events; not only to feel they are part of a community of parents who have been through the same – but also to put their child's name out there, to make these small lives significant and known to many, because only then can there be any fragment of sense or meaning.

One of the developments over recent years that has made the sharing of parents' stories possible has been the internet. Social media has made a big difference to the isolation bereaved parents can feel. It offers parents the opportunity to connect with other bereaved parents across the world, and those whose children have died from unusual and rare diseases can find others who have had children with the same condition. And because these connections are across the globe there is usually someone ready to listen at all times of day or night. This online community offers a compassion and camaraderie that crosses cultures. For some parents the online support is an invaluable replacement for the groups they had relied on whilst their child was alive: people they had known in the outpatient clinics and on the wards.

Through either creating a personal site where their child's story is told, pictures are shared and updates are given, or linking to an already established site (often websites organisations connected with childhood illnesses or bereavement have their own remembrance pages), parents safely place their child where, despite them no longer having a physical presence, others still meet and want to know about them, and where parents can carry on talking about them and know that their relationship with them is still part of who they are.

Chapter 11

WORKING AS A COUNSELLOR WITH BEREAVED PARENTS

...actually this [never being able to find a substitute for a loss] is how it should be. It is the only way of perpetuating the love we do not wish to relinquish.

Sigmund Freud, after the death of his daughter
Sophie, in personal correspondence to a
friend whose son had recently died

For her doctorate Denise Turner, a former social worker, researched the experiences of parents whose child had died suddenly and unexpectedly at home (Turner 2014b). She had herself experienced the loss of her son, Joe, at the age of nineteen months in these circumstances, and her thesis movingly links the personal with the academic. What she records about the morning she found that Joe had died in his cot at home is that the paramedic who arrived on her doorstep following her call to the emergency services was brusque and clumsy, and the police officers who followed left her feeling undermined, disbelieved and threatened, rendering an already traumatic experience unimaginably terrible. She writes that her main concern in that moment was for her other two children, Joe's twin Dan and her daughter Amy. She needed Amy, as an older child, to be protected from what was happening, and wanted to get her away from the house and to school. But she had to fight to be allowed out of the house. Later experiences with the coroner, the registrar who registered Joe's death and the health visitor were no easier or kinder:

> That remains one of my lasting impressions of Joe's death. That most of the professionals involved were having a terrible time. No one seemed genuinely able to cope. The horror of the situation, the fear of being held culpable and the sheer randomness of the death seemed to immobilize people's basic humanity at this most human of times. (Turner 2014b, p.31)

Turner's interviews with nine other parents suddenly bereaved in this way showed that she had not been alone in this. Because, thankfully, sudden and unexpected infant death is becoming increasingly rare, professionals who are exposed to it, despite their training, can become deskilled, clumsy and anxious. It was interesting to read in her account that universally the professionals the parents in this study found the most sensitive and the least defensive were funeral directors. Their familiarity with death allows a calm and competence that brings a welcome relief.

My colleague and I occasionally saw parents who had experienced a sudden and unexpected infant death in the home, but not often. And we certainly met parents whose experience of the professionals involved was a positive one. But the reason I am beginning this chapter by including Turner's study is because I think it is important to acknowledge how difficult it can be for most of us to be who we need to be around child death. And remembering that is helpful when we think about all the professionals parents will be encountering after their child has died, whether suddenly and unexpectedly or because of an accident or illness: GPs, teachers, social workers, health visitors, coroners and their staff, and counsellors, to name a few.

When I started working with bereaved parents I had already been a counsellor for twenty years, mostly working in a doctor's surgery. Before that I was a social worker in mental health. I came to the job with a lot of experience of counselling and of working within the NHS. But I learned very quickly that this work was different. In the first week my induction included a morning in the mortuary, a visit to local funeral directors, and attending the funerals held by the chaplains for all the babies miscarried or born so prematurely that they were too young to be registered.

I was introduced to the book of remembrance in the chapel where parents can choose to record their child's death, and shown how to remove pages so that new names could be inscribed. I was shown the bereavement boxes that are kept on all the paediatric wards, and learned how it would be my responsibility to ensure that the contents were complete: ink pads for handprints, a disposable camera for photographs, tiny folders with a plastic wallet to hold a lock of hair. I walked the route from the paediatric intensive care ward to the mortuary which avoided too many encounters with the public. And I attended my first ward round where I became dazed and troubled by all the ways a small child could become very sick. It was a new and disconcerting world, one I hadn't known anything about before, and I dreaded the first call coming when I would be asked to meet a parent who had lost a child.

I am remembering this time because it helps me not to feel critical when I read about professionals who struggle, like those Denise Turner encountered. I would have been just the same. It also puts me back in touch with the strange and terrifying world parents encounter when they first come into contact with the hospital.

I was helped by my experienced colleague and my excellent supervisor, and by time passing and familiarity. I also discovered within me a compassion for the parents and children I was meeting, which I admit had begun to run a little dry in my work in the GP practice. Here were people who were facing the worst time of their lives and I wanted to be alongside them.

But I was impacted by what I was experiencing, and we all are. Death has become the great taboo, no longer happening within our homes and our communities, but medicalised and removed. For many of us, until we experience the loss of someone close to us, our only contact with death will have been through what we have read or seen in films or on the television. So often these portrayals of death are sentimentalised, sanitised and romanticised or, at the other extreme, sensationalised and horrific. When we come up against death that is random, tragic, unjust and untimely, as the death of a child inevitably is, we are shaken to the core. There is something profoundly unsettling about the extraordinariness of what is happening in the context of an ordinary life.

I imagined that with all the exposure I had through my work, I would have become resilient. But recently I read *The Violet Hour* by Sergio del Molino, an account of his beloved son Pablo's death before he reached the age of two (del Molino 2013). Del Molino is unsparing in the descriptions he gives of his and his wife's suffering. Whilst reading this book I had a dream I had not had for twenty years. I dreamed I had lost my son. He was as small as a piece of Lego, and I had left him in the care of someone I later realised had not noticed him, because he was so small. I returned and looked for him everywhere, searching through boxes of non-living Lego trying to find my boy. I was desperate and woke up shaken and sweating. How vulnerable we parents are to having those deeply held fears of loss triggered, even when our children are now parents themselves.

As a counsellor in this new setting I soon learned that I would need to modify, and to a degree discard, some of the beliefs and principles I had previously held, especially those to do with boundaries, how sessions are agreed and arranged, and the consistency of session length and location. I am sure this is the experience of all counsellors working in hospitals and in hospices or with adults or children who are sick.

I have already written about how important it was to be flexible and responsive when it came to arranging counselling sessions. It was not helpful or appropriate to arrange a contract from the start for a fixed number of sessions. Rarely was it helpful or realistic to rigidly stick to a regular session at the same time each week. When parents are looking after a sick child at home it is impossible for them to know from one week to the next what their lives will be like. And in the early weeks and months after their child has died, whilst some parents welcome the security a regular counselling appointment brings, others are reluctant to make a commitment at a time when they are feeling so emotionally overwhelmed.

Sometimes telephone appointments were a better way of providing a service, although it took me time to learn how to be fully present to a parent who was not in the same physical space as I was. I found it difficult to manage silences, and the times when there were no words to say I had to resist offering platitudes and reassurances or solutions. I also learned that on the phone a fifty-minute session is too long for me to be fully attentive. So I shortened the time.

Jane's daughter Ivy has a life-limiting condition and Jane is her full-time carer. She and I spoke on the phone fortnightly for over a year, usually timing the call for when Ivy was at school. But when Ivy was too unwell for school Jane and I would have to snatch what time we could. I only met Jane in person once, when Ivy had a brief inpatient stay at the hospital, but over the year we developed a good connection.

In my last week at the hospital I received a call from Mike, a father whom I had seen regularly in the past, but with whom I had been having telephone sessions for the previous year. This was because his son Theo had become too unwell for his father to feel comfortable leaving him in the care of others in order to come to the hospital. Mike and Theo's mother were divorced and Mike was Theo's full-time carer. Mike was calling me to let me know that Theo was now in the local hospital and nearing the end of his life.

So my last session with Mike was not in the counselling room, nor on the phone, but in a small room of the local hospital at Theo's bedside. Here Mike and Theo's mother were keeping vigil. It was not a time for talking but just to be there. And it was challenging for me. This was a final meeting with a parent I had known for some time. It was no longer a confidential meeting; we were in the presence of his former wife and his dying son. Occasionally nurses were in the room with us. In no way could the focus be on Mike's needs and feelings, but only on Theo. It was a bitter ending for me. I knew I would not see Mike again and that I was leaving at possibly the hardest time for him. There was nothing textbook about this ending.

Theo died the next day – my final day at the hospital.

However, most of the work with parents was in the privacy of the counselling room, which was in a separate building from the main hospital, a short distance from the children's wards. If their child was an inpatient, parents would tell me they valued the short walk and the geographical separation this gave them from the busy, noisy ward and all the emotions that were being played out there. Understandably parents would only come if they felt comfortable leaving their child for a while; perhaps another family member took their place on the ward, or they knew their child was sleeping. But rarely would a parent be able to engage fully in the session without the reassuring presence of their phone, turned on and placed on the table between us. The session could always be interrupted; their child was uppermost in mind.

Not all parents were comfortable leaving their child on the ward and this meant I would need to go to them. Sometimes we would be able to find a quiet space on the ward if a single room happened to be vacant, but more often we would only have the limited privacy that drawn curtains and soft voices allow. Then there was always the possibility of being interrupted by medical staff or visitors, which meant that confidentiality and explanations about who I was and why I was there had to be negotiated rather quickly. It is also important to say that if parents had been waiting all day, or possibly several days, to see the consultant, and the consultant arrived during the time I had arranged to meet them on the ward, our commitment was no longer sacrosanct. It was time for me to step aside.

I also had to address the issue of the child being present during the counselling. For children who were of an age to understand the conversations, this was out of the question, although a parent's view of when this might be and my feelings about it did not always tally. This is understandable. When a parent is desperate to talk, and many difficult conversations have already been held in their child's presence, boundaries, out of necessity, will have become more relaxed.

But with infants and babies it was possible, although the child's presence still made a difference to the work. Inevitably the parent would be less focused on our conversation. Their attention would be distracted from time to time as they were drawn to check on their child, to soothe or simply to acknowledge the child was there in the room with us. And a distressed parent might hold back on expressing feelings in front of their child, whatever their age.

I had to manage my own feelings about being in the presence of a child who was suffering, and yet attend fully to their parent. When I met a parent for the first time and a child was present, I found it more comfortable to first introduce myself to the parent(s) and, having engaged with them, ask their permission to say hello to their child, if I hadn't already been invited to by the parent. I would check out what the parent would like me to call their child, as often the name on the referral or the medical notes wasn't the familiar name by which the child was known. Whatever age the child was, I would tell them my name and explain that I was there to talk to their parent.

Parents' experience in the hospital will have been that attention was almost exclusively on their child and they would not have wanted it any other way. But it was important that as the counsellor I was different. I was there for the parent, and only if invited.

The first time I met Carly, Bryony's mother, she was sitting next to her daughter's cot on the ward. She spoke to me but would not look at me. Her whole attention was on her daughter who was sleeping in the cot and who was dying. Carly held Bryony's coat on her lap. She told me that she would not leave Bryony until she could put her in her coat and take her home. This was not likely to happen, and I think Carly knew that. But I learned to respect parents' degree of readiness to allow themselves to admit both to themselves and others that their child was dying. This is not about denial but timing. It is also about hope, and the need to hold tightly to a fragile glimmer of light in so much darkness, however unrealistic that might be. There is an old Spanish saying – 'Lo último que muere es la esperanza': 'Hope dies last.'

In this work I had to learn how to be in the presence of a child who had died, something counselling training and experience had not prepared me for. But then, I am not sure anything could. There were times when I knew the child, because I had been working with their parents and had met the child on the ward. Other times neither the parents nor their child were known to me: we had not met before, but the parents had asked to see a counsellor. Looking back, I think this influenced how I handled entering the room where parents and child were. If the parents were known to me, I would reach out to them first, and then take my cue from them about when I would acknowledge their child. If the parents were strangers, I would acknowledge their child first, softly saying hello, always referring to the child by name, before turning to the parents to introduce myself and express my sympathy. I am sure everyone has their own way of managing this. What I found was important for me was to be clear for myself how I was going to be before I entered the room.

At this time the parents, counsellor and any others present, possibly family and hospital staff, are all in a transitional period. The child is still a very real physical presence; they are still of this world, even though they have passed into another. It is a profound moment. It is never a time for counselling, but only to be present; to bear witness to the tragedy before us. Parents for whom I was able to be there in this way, and who subsequently came to me for counselling, would sometimes refer to it and to the importance for them that I had met with their child at that moment. It was always significant for me too.

One day I received a call from a ward asking me to meet with a couple whose baby son had died earlier that morning. It was an unexpected death and the couple had come from quite a distance away. They wanted to see me before they returned home. I suggested they came to see me in the counselling room, or on the ward if that was easier. However, they asked to meet me in the hospital coffee shop. I expressed my concern that this was a noisy, public place, but this was what they wanted. So we met there and we talked about their baby and the plans they were making about letting his older sister and the family know. They seemed calm and not at all distracted by our busy surroundings. They explained that they had cared for their baby until it had been time for him to be taken to the mortuary, and then they needed to be in 'an ordinary place'. What had felt extraordinary to me had felt ordinary to them, and being there felt right. I think I could understand that.

Much of what I learned about being with children and their parents when a child had just died was from the nurses on the wards. They were the people who gently assisted the children as they journeyed from life to death, showing parents how to hold and perform simple tasks for them, to help them feel calm and comfortable; modelling how normal and important it is to keep on speaking to a child who has died; and suggesting to parents that they might want to bathe and dress their child before they take them to the mortuary. The nursing staff were sensitive, appropriate and resilient in ways that never failed to impress and move me.

I also learned from the mortuary team, for whom I developed enormous admiration. They based their whole approach to the work on the principle that when patients were placed in their care they remained patients until they left the mortuary. They were never referred to as a 'body'. Parents were able to spend time with their child in the mortuary in what was called the viewing room. Here, before the parent came in, mortuary staff would place the child in an appropriately sized cot or bed with a child's coverlet. There were comfortable chairs for parents who wanted to hold their child again, and they were given privacy. When they were ready to leave they placed their child back on the bed, rang a bell to let staff know they were leaving and left the room. Only then would the mortuary staff enter and return the child to the mortuary refrigerator. Parents would tell me how much they appreciated this respectful treatment of them and their child.

A very useful and thorough resource available to parents is a book produced by the charity Children's Cancer and Leukaemia Group, which is available to download online. *Facing the Death of Your Child* is written by a clinical psychologist and a bereaved parent. It addresses openly and honestly what can be so hard for parents who know their child is going to die to ask questions about: questions such as how to talk about dying to their child, how to be with their child in their final hours and what the end can be like (Edwards and Palmer 2015).

In my work with parents whose children were on the wards, often very sick and sometimes coming to the end of their lives, I was part of a large and often confusingly complex team of professionals. But critically there was something different about my role. My first responsibility was to the parents, not the child, and the parents were not patients of the hospital.

When I was a counsellor in a GP surgery my clients were the patients of the practice. I shared a duty of care for them with the rest of the medical team, wrote in the medical notes and had a responsibility to communicate with my colleagues about them, especially if I had a concern about their wellbeing. In the hospital the notes were in the child's name and what I knew or learned about their parents' fears and fragilities did not belong there. Ward staff would sometimes pass on information to me about parents which I would have preferred to have learned from them myself, and at times I would be holding information about parents which I did not feel was helpful or my place to share with other staff. Because I was the only member of the team not writing in the notes regularly, I sometimes worried that colleagues might be wondering whether I was doing anything!

However concerned ward staff might be about a parent, if that parent did not want to see me they had every right not to. Conversely, I knew that everyone I saw was choosing to see me, though sometimes it could have been because they were too polite to refuse or wanted to be compliant.

This being on the margins was, I think, helpful to parents, who would see me as someone set apart from the intensity, complexities and uncertainties of the ward. Nonetheless they found it reassuring to know that I had a direct line to the medical team, and would be able to ask questions or speak up on their behalf when they were feeling worried or confused. This connection became even more valuable once their child was no longer an inpatient, either because they had been discharged, or died. I had an e-mail address and a direct phone line.

Working in a hospital meant that as a counsellor I would not only encounter parents on the wards or in the counselling room. I would find that I was queuing behind them in the hospital supermarket, we would be singing carols together on the ward at Christmas, or they would see me call by and meet with another parent on the ward or have a conversation with one of the nurses. There were times when I would hold their child if I was on the ward and they were called away, when I would comfort their child if she became distressed and she and I would talk to each other. The parents' lives and mine overlapped, and it was important that both they and I found ways of being comfortable with that. Some parents would become colleagues when they agreed to be speakers at the study days we arranged for staff.

One of the most challenging times for me as a counsellor was when I facilitated the group for bereaved parents, as this would be attended by some parents who I was seeing individually or as a couple for counselling, others who had seen my colleague, and parents who had not come for counselling. This meant that there were some who felt they had a special relationship with me, some to whom I was unfamiliar and others who I feared were comparing me unfavourably to my colleague! I knew some of the parents' stories better than others and I also knew what they were choosing not to talk about. Perhaps hardest of all was the time when one parent I had seen individually told the group something she had understood me to say, and I was horrified. It was not what I had meant to say at all...but neither was it appropriate for me to question it in the group. My co-facilitator told me afterwards that although I had not said anything, the expression in my eyes had given away rather more.

So our lives overlapped and the edges of my role became permeable, but I found that as a counsellor I was comfortable with being what felt to be more real. These were counselling relationships that demanded warmth and human responsiveness over anything else.

I was strongly resistant to calling the work I did with parents whose child had died bereavement counselling. Certainly for those I had been supporting whilst their child was still alive it would have been meaningless for the counselling to suddenly now have this label attached. But for the others, too, those whose child I had not known in life, it rarely felt right.

I wonder if this is because when the word 'counselling' has an adjective preceding it, the adjective usually identifies a problem the client is dealing with: debt counselling, addiction counselling, stress counselling. Bereavement is not a problem. It happens to all of us. It is part of the stuff of our lives even when it is untimely and tragic. Some people who have been bereaved seek counselling. But using the word 'bereavement' to describe the work that goes on between a counsellor and someone who is grieving reduces it, limits it and somehow makes it all too bland and clichéd. I wonder if that is why some parents who experience the loss of their child refuse to see a counsellor. They fear their muddle and terror, their emptiness and their longing might somehow be forced into a shape that is manageable and safe but sterile and over-simplified.

When I was a counsellor in general practice I was referred clients who were dealing with any number of problems, amongst them anxiety, depression, loneliness and ill health. They came to see me with a hope that after talking through their problems they might feel a sense of relief, a better understanding of the way they were feeling and possibly some strategies for managing. The parents I saw at the hospital for counselling came with no such agenda. Usually they came because someone had suggested it might be a good idea. Sometimes they came because they had been seeing me before their child's death, and so continuing the conversation felt appropriate and a good idea. But no parent came to me because they wanted to feel better. Their pain was what was now underscoring their relationship with their child.

Returning to Denise Turner, with whom I began this chapter: Denise didn't want to see a counsellor after her son Joe died. She became acutely aware that there were a number of expectations about how bereaved parents should behave: how they should dress, what they should do and refrain from doing, and along with that was a view that they should see a bereavement counsellor. But what she wanted was practical support. She chose to speak to a psychologist on the phone, because her main concern was to get it right for her daughter Amy, and his advice was all she needed at that time. He suggested that if she was 'all right', then Amy would be too. 'The psychologist's telephone edict that I should "be all right" became the magnetic north I followed in trying to protect them [Amy and Joe's twin brother Dan] from the aftermath of Joe's death' (Turner 2014a, p.33).

For almost all the parents my colleague and I saw, counselling was valuable, but there are many who lose a child and find ways of becoming 'all right' through means other than counselling. Friends, faith, new directions, children, travel, writing, art...all are ways of integrating the loss and allowing it to find a place where over time it ceases to burn with such intensity. Then they can begin to rebuild their lives in this world and with the beloved child for whom they grieve.

Final thoughts

Christopher saw me for counselling over a period of three years. He had had a very close relationship with his son Marcus who had died at the age of ten. Marcus had complex needs, learning disabilities and suffered frequent seizures. His parents shared his care, each working part time to make this possible. Christopher identified not long after Marcus's death that he would find counselling helpful. Unlike his wife Jasmine, Christopher wanted to talk about Marcus a lot. Jasmine found talking upsetting and preferred to mourn him privately. Christopher understood this, and by coming to counselling met his own needs to talk, and protected and supported Jasmine in her needs too.

At the beginning of every session, Christopher would tell me how he wanted to remember Marcus that day. He would sometimes bring a photograph or a piece of art work, sometimes a significant piece of music, things that would connect him with his son for that hour. Then he would begin to talk, sometimes with tears and other times taking pleasure in remembering. It was a privilege to be part of this.

One week Christopher had been talking about a holiday spent with Jasmine and Marcus at the seaside. He was remembering the beach, the gulls, the sandwiches they ate and the colour of Marcus's sweater. Then he apologised to me for rambling.

The word 'rambling' produced in me a strong and happy association. There is nothing I enjoy more than rambling, walking slowly and thoughtfully through the countryside, often with a friend, pausing to take in the world around me, and sharing and storing up memories. Then I understood that this was the kind of rambling Christopher was doing with me. And our companion was Marcus.

REFERENCES

Bowlby, J. (1980) *Attachment and Loss Vol. 3. Loss: Sadness and Depression.* New York: Basic Books.

Brierley-Jones, L., Crawley, R., Lomax, S. and Ayers, S. (2014–2015) 'Stillbirth and stigma: The spoiling and repair of multiple social identities.' *OMEGA – Journal of Death and Dying 70*, 2, 143–168.

Chalmers, A. (2007) 'A Family's Journey.' In P. Sidebotham and P. Fleming (eds) *Unexpected Death in Childhood.* London: John Wiley & Sons.

Cohen, M. (2003) *Sent Before My Time: A Child Psychotherapist's View of Life on a Neonatal Intensive Care Unit.* The Tavistock Clinic Series. London: H. Karnac (Books) Ltd.

Cote-Arsenault, D. and O'Leary, J. (2015) 'Understanding the Experience of Pregnancy Subsequent to a Perinatal Loss.' In P. Wright, R. Limbo and P. Black (eds) *Perinatal and Pediatric Bereavement.* New York: Springer Publishing.

Cote-Arsenault, D., Krowchuk, H., Hall, W.J. and Denney-Koelsch, E. (2015) 'We want what's best for our baby: Prenatal parenting of babies with lethal conditions.' *Journal of Prenatal and Perinatal Psychology and Health 29*, 3, 157–176. Available at www.ncbi.nlm.nih.gov/pmc/articles/PMC4652586 (accessed 13 April 2017).

Crawley, R., Lomax, S. and Ayers, S. (2013) 'Recovering from stillbirth: The effects of making and sharing memories on maternal health.' *Journal of Reproductive and Infant Psychology 31*, 195–207.

del Molino, S. (2013) *The Violet Hour.* Madrid: Hispabooks Publishing.

Edwards, L. and Palmer, J. (2015) *Facing the Death of Your Child: Suggestions and Help for Families, Before and After.* Leicester: Children's Cancer and Leukaemia Group and The Royal Marsden NHS Trust.

Fogle, M. (2015) 'Grief crashes over you like a tidal wave.' *Times 2*, 19 October, pp.2–3.

Greene, J. (2016) 'Oh my son, I love you but I will never be the father I was before your sister died.' *The Sunday Times*, 30 October, p.22.

Hindmarch, C. (2009) *On the Death of a Child* (3rd edition). Oxford: Radcliffe Publishing.

Keane, H. (2009) 'Foetal personhood and representations of the absent child in pregnancy loss memorialization.' *Feminist Theory 102*, 153–171.

Marsh, H. (2014) *Do No Harm: Stories of Life, Death and Brain Surgery.* London: Weidenfeld and Nicolson.

McLaren, J. (1998) 'A new understanding of grief: A counsellor's perspective.' *Mortality 3*, 3, 275–290.

Riches, G. and Dawson, P. (2000) *An Intimate Loneliness: Supporting Bereaved Parents and Siblings*. Buckingham: Open University Press.

Roberts, T. (2015) 'Cancer in children.' *Observer Magazine*, 15 November, pp.31–35.

Turner, D. (2014a) '"Memories are made of this": Personal reflections on the creation and maintenance of memorials and mementoes.' *Bereavement Care 35*, 3, 92–96.

Turner, D. (2014b) 'Telling the Story: What can be Learned from Parents' Experience of the Professional Response following the Sudden, Unexpected Death of a Child.' Doctoral thesis, University of Sussex.

Walter, T. (2011) 'Angels not souls: Popular religion in the online mourning for British celebrity Jade Goody.' *Religion 41*, 1, 29–51.

Walter, T. (2016) 'The dead who become angels: Bereavement and vernacular religion.' *OMEGA – Journal of Death and Dying 73*, 1, 3–28.

Winnicott, D.W. (1990) *The Maturational Processes and the Facilitating Environment*. London: Karnac Books.

Winnicott, D.W. (2000) *The Child, the Family and the Outside World*. London: Penguin Random House.

Yalom, I.D. with Leszcz, M. (2005) *The Theory and Practice of Group Psychotherapy* (5th edition). New York: Basic Books. (Original work published 1975.)

RESOURCES

A Child of Mine
A charity led by bereaved parents offering practical information, guidance and support to parents following the death of their child.

www.achildofmine.org.uk

Bliss
Offers support for families where babies have been born prematurely and/or unwell.

www.bliss.org.uk

Child Bereavement UK
Gives support to families when a baby or child of any age dies or is dying, or when a child faces bereavement, and also provides education and training for those working in the field.

www.childbereavementuk.org

Child Death Helpline
A helpline staffed by volunteer parents who have themselves suffered the loss of a child, offering support to anyone affected by the death of a child of any age, however recent or long ago.

Freephone: 0800 282 986/0808 800 6019

www.childdeathhelpline.org.uk

Childhood Bereavement Network
An organisation for those working with bereaved children, young people and their families across the UK.

www.childhoodbereavementnetwork.org.uk

Children of Jannah
A charity supporting Muslim parents following the death of their child or baby.

www.childrenofjannah.com

Children's Cancer and Leukaemia Group

Gives information, resources and support to families where there is a child who has cancer and to professionals involved in their treatment and care.

www.cclg.org.uk

MAMA Academy

Provides information to pregnant women and their health care professionals in order to raise awareness of baby loss, improve antenatal health and reduce stillbirth and neonatal death.

www.mamaacademy.org.uk

Meningitis Now

The UK's largest meningitis charity, offering support to families, funding research and raising awareness.

www.meningitisnow.org

Neuroblastoma UK

A charity which funds research into neuroblastoma, an aggressive childhood cancer, working towards developing treatments that are more effective and also kinder to children's bodies.

www.neuroblastoma.org.uk

Rainbow Trust

Provides practical, financial and emotional support to families where a child has a life-threatening or life-limiting illness.

www.rainbowtrust.org.uk

Sands

A stillbirth and neonatal death charity which gives support to anyone affected by the death of a baby, works to improve the care bereaved parents receive and promotes research into stillbirth and neonatal death.

www.uk-sands.org

The Compassionate Friends

An organisation of bereaved family members who offer support to others who have suffered the loss of a child and work to raise awareness of the issues around child death.

www.tcf.org.uk

Together for Short Lives

A children's hospice charity which gives help and advice to families and professionals, and works with them to ensure children with life-shortening conditions have the best care and quality of life possible, and the best end-of-life care.

www.togetherforshortlives.org.uk

Winston's Wish

Provides specialist child bereavement support services for families and professionals.

www.winstonswish.org.uk